POWER
THOUGHTS

THE GIFT OF ADVERSITY

BERT RODRIGUEZ

BALBOA.
PRESS

A DIVISION OF HAY HOUSE

Balboa Press books may be ordered through booksellers or by contacting:

Balboa Press
A Division of Hay House
1663 Liberty Drive
Bloomington, IN 47403
www.balboapress.com
1 (877) 407-4847

Print information available on the last page.

ISBN: 978-1-5043-7668-6 (sc)
ISBN: 978-1-5043-7669-3 (e)

Balboa Press rev. date: 04/18/2017

Table of Contents

Acknowledgements

I want to thank all those that confided in me and allowed me to share my perspective on what they were facing in their lives with them. It was that interaction that brought out and created these Power Thoughts.

Thank you to Victoria Roman and VK Graphics for the superb work on the illustration graphics layouts.

My friends who helped:

Bruce Hogman who graciously took on the task of editing, corrections, suggestions and ideas to help my thoughts and words take on a more reader friendly style that gives it the necessary flow in its final stage.

And lastly, this whole project would not have gotten to this point without an individual who I have always considered my brother and dearest friend. He has motivated me, advised me, convinced me to make some important and crucial changes, has shared his resources for marketing, website builders, editing and other important connection's in this process, Stevie Moon.

About the Author

"The strength and success of anything you do is limited only by how much you are willing to sacrifice yourself in order to succeed."

—Bert Rodriguez

Bert Rodriguez dedicated over sixty years to the study and understanding of our bodies, both the physical and mental aspects, and the ability to control and use these to experience this adventure we call life. From early childhood, he has been on a journey to comprehend how our thoughts, emotions and attitudes strongly influence our physical being and, in turn, our lives, who we become, our purpose and the final product of what we create and are able to share with our children, others and future generations.

These short thoughts and quotes he shares with all of you form an effective philosophy that he studied and applied to his own life, family, as well as the lives of those he counseled through the years. They address some of the things we all have or will encounter in different ways. These are simple, yet powerful words, that give you the opportunity to gain a different perspective on how to combine and be in harmony with the challenges, obstacles and struggles we all face in our lives.

The narrative of this book will show you how to value them with a different perspective and mindset of acceptance and flow, rather than one of resistance and confrontation. In order to avoid stress, and the illnesses and problems it can cause, we must acquire the ability to understand and accept who we are and how to appreciate and control every aspect of our minds and internal emotions. Studying and contemplating on these Power Thoughts will help you discover and understand yourself better, as well as the people around you. We are all different and yet all the same when it comes to how we can deal with what happens in our daily lives. You are not alone.

With these Power Thoughts, Bert expresses a mindset he acquired through personal experience. These thoughts he learned through trial and error with decisions he made that resulted in both great successes and devastating failures. They are hard earned lessons he used, to personally overcome situations. He is certain they can help guide you to conquer life's inevitable and numerous obstacles while empowering you with a solid foundation on how to redirect yourself to a contented state of mind and a positive future.

You will find his book useful in helping you strengthen your resolve and level of commitment to overcoming difficulties.

Bert ran the gamut of situations and range of emotions from being raised by a loving family to the lowest emotions of leaving home at thirteen, being a major drug dealer in Miami during the Scarface era, addicted to heroin for fifteen years, being homeless, facing a number of close encounters with death including being shot by police, being incarcerated, was forced to experience the horror of kicking a heroin and cocaine addiction without medication while incarcerated, returning to a life of drugs and crime and finally finding the strength and courage to for the second time break a heroin addiction and finally making up his mind then to realize a hard and honest assessment of himself, understand the decisions and course his life had taken and then finding the strength inside himself to straighten out his life and become the person he knew he wanted and was meant to be.

Bert earned black belts in eight distinct styles of martial arts, including four master degrees. As a result, he has extensive knowledge of the foundations, backgrounds, histories and philosophies of Zen, harmony as well as the application to life.

He later trained members of the United States Drug Enforcement Administration, Metro Dade Police Academy, Broward County Sheriff's Office, and numerous individuals in various departments in the US military and armed forces.

Bert decided to become a consummate life coach. He mentored and helped his students and clients know themselves, face their fears and empower themselves to achieve success in their individual fields. He inspired others.

He is fortunate to have acquired an extensive background as a counselor and motivational speaker in the fields of positive attitude, self-hypnosis and personal motivation.

His reputation in kickboxing and boxing, both amateur and professional, elevated him to become a highly respected trainer of world champions.

He used lessons learned from his experiences and hardships to become a successful entrepreneur through strength of character and a high level of commitment to overcoming difficulties.

Bert established Power Punch Promotions in South Florida, which opened and owned US #1 Fitness Centers in West Palm Beach, North Miami, and Dania Beach, Florida, and US #1 Business Systems and Investments.

He appeared in and been featured on radio and television shows and networks, including 20/20, Dateline, CNN, NBC, CNBC, BBC, PBS, the Learning Channel, the Discovery Channel, Canadian Broadcasting, Telemundo, Univision, and others worldwide.

Bert's life experiences brought him to share with you what can benefit you in whatever particular situation you need or want to overcome and achieve success in. He wrote and published two books – *Face Fear Create Courage*, which describe in detail the exciting adventure of his life's ups and downs and also *Power Thoughts - Motivational Fuel for Success*, which is a collection of quotes to encourage, inspire, motivate, and empower readers to reach their highest potential in whatever goal they choose for their lives. He continues sharing these motivational and empowering thoughts with this sequel, *Power Thoughts – The Gift of Adversity*, that will give you a way to turn your obstacles and challenges to benefits and opportunities. It is his deepest desire that you find them to be of service and useful to you in following your Yellow Brick Road and always finding the silver lining in your life.

May you always follow the advice of a statement used by as a very physically small and yet powerful and successful individual Grace Mary Hopper, whose motto was "Dare and Do". The US Navy honored ADM Hopper by naming the guided missile destroyer DDG-70 USS Hopper for her, as well as holding a final retirement service for her aboard the USS Constitution in Boston Harbor, the oldest active duty battleship in the fleet.

—Bruce Hogman MA, MEd

REVIEW

"After I read Master Bert's new book I realized a few things. First I am definitely going to re-read it and take more notes. Secondly I do not think, short of the Bible have I read a more succinct collection of thoughts, ideas and answers as to how to balance and conduct one's life. It is very practically written that will appeal to everyone and as you read through it, everything makes complete sense. Then you realize that you are not doing all of these things and if you started to, your life and how you felt about yourself would markedly improve. One thing the two of us have in common is experiencing a medical situation where we both faced very serious issues that could have causes permanent damage. We both fought back physically, mentally and spiritually to overcome these medical setbacks. This book is one that can change your life if you take the time to read it. It is an easy read and I had trouble putting it down. Do not miss this amazing opportunity to learn from what Master Bert has written here. You will never look at your world and self the same – ONLY BETTER"!!

Dr. E. Thomas Arne, Jr., D.O., FACC. Medical Director Gulfshore Personalized Care, Past Medical Director Sarasota Memorial Hospital Congestive Heart Failure Program, Past Assistant Professor of Medicine at Michigan State University.

Introduction

In the final weeks of completing the draft for this book, I experienced a terrible yet beneficial detour in what has been a roller-coaster ride of a life. On my way to visit my mom in Lockwood Missouri, as I did a flight roulette of changes from Ft. Lauderdale to Washington to O'Hara to Dallas to Springfield, I was told that my flight from Dallas to Springfield was cancelled until the next morning and that I would have to wait overnight at the airport, my ability to go with the flow was tested to the limit. After accepting the circumstances and hopping on the plane to Dallas, I sat down to read and spend the time in peaceful meditation.

I didn't realize life had another slight detour planned for me. Sitting in a tight squeeze in the last row window seat on the flight to Dallas, I felt my left hand and arm falling asleep. Thinking That I may have been lying on it and restricted the blood flow, I shook it, slapped it and moved it around to try and get the circulation going. As I reached up to turn on the light I also noticed I couldn't raise it, control it to push the light button. As my leg and foot also felt a numb tingling feeling I suspected something else was evidently taking place. Having read, when my mom had a quadruple bypass four years earlier, that these could be signs of a heart malfunction, yet always being in perfect health throughout my life other than occasional high blood pressure, I none the less began to feel I was having a stroke. Not wanting to create a commotion and having forty-five minutes to land in Dallas I tried coughing and deep breathing to see if I could clear my head.

We landed and being in the last seat in the back I waited for the entire plane to empty before I tried to stand up. That didn't go all too well, since I had lost total control and feeling of the left side of my body.

I then decided to tell the stewardess that I thought I was having a stroke. She told me to remain seated, brought me some water and told me she would call the paramedics. I remained as calm as I could under the circumstances and waited. When they arrived they took my blood pressure which was 240/120 confirmed that I was indeed having a stroke and sped me off to The Zale Lipchy University Hospital, a stroke specialist unit of the UT Southwestern Medical Center in Dallas.

Upon arriving, they asked me if I would be willing to take a new drug called CPA that could only be administered within the first four hours of the sign of a stroke and could reduce the damage done. Of course I agreed and within fifteen minutes the feeling and control of my left hand and side from toes to cheek returned to normal. Unfortunately it only lasted for 20 minutes and once again I lost total control and coordination. As the Dr. told me to touch his finger with my left index finger my hand would go into an uncontrollable spastic array of flapping movements. I began to worry but did my best to keep a game face and good attitude. They took me in for a brain scan as well as an MRI and found that indeed I had had two, what they referred to as mini strokes, one on either side of my brain.

They also discovered that the carotid arteries on either side of my neck were clogged with plaque, one ninety five percent, the other sixty five percent. For the next six days as they prepared to operate on the worse one first all I could do was try my best to on my own try somehow to reconnect my brain to the left side of my body by moving it as best I could, specially my fingers and hand which had become totally useless.

As I sat there for the following ten days contemplating on this misfortune and seeing some of the other patients and how crippling the effects of a stroke can be, I immediately tried to implement the attitude that I have had since early youth and always experienced throughout my life of the law of Ying and Yang that everything is always as good as it is bad, depending on your perspective.

That, and the fact that, as I stated in my first book, I have felt throughout my life that God and a Universal Force has always carried me through adversities as well as numerous close calls with death to fulfill a purpose greater than myself as a individual, I would turn this whole event to my advantage. Not only did I land in Dallas where a hospital specializing in strokes and with the finest Doctors, nurses and care, but also that as the doctor mentioned, had I not had the two smaller strokes first, the clogged arteries which were discovered because of them would have certainly done me in.

I also feel that it has given me the chance one more time in my life to walk the talk and practice what I preach. It's easy to give advice about facing challenges, obstacles and problems when they are happening to someone else or when we have no emotional, mental or physical attachment or connection, but a totally different situation when we are living the experiences ourselves in real time.

I always carry copies of both my books to share with others, *Face Fear Create Courage*, which relates my adventures with challenges and adversities including close brushes with death but also my second book *Power Thoughts- Motivational Fuel For Success*, that has quotes that speak of the philosophy that has carried me to personal successes in spite of everything I have had to confront and overcome. While lying there in the hospital, I constantly read and re-read the passages in order to constantly let the power of my thoughts send the right healing endorphins into my body and not let the negative side of the circumstance prevent me from helping the body's natural and miraculous healing resources to help me recuperate.

As I write this, I am on my fourth week of this most scary and horrid experience and am working through my physical and mental strengthening therapy to regain my total health. I have no doubt I will be one hundred percent and actually better and stronger from having gone through and survived this most devastating, and, to say the least, unpleasant situation.

I hope that my experience as well as the thoughts and philosophy I share with you in this and in my previous books help strengthen and carry you through whatever you may confront or have to overcome in your life's journey.

I wholeheartedly and firmly believe that the two most important and valuable assets that we will ever possess are our physical and mental health! Our ability to understand, strengthen, nourish, and improve our capabilities to use them is crucial to our survival and growth.

At an early age, I became intrigued with the power of the mind, as well as the effects of a good diet, to promote proper physical growth and strength. In later years, while being involved with the fitness business, as well as training athletes, competitors and world champions, I realized a correlation exists between proper physical nutrition and mental nutrition. In both cases, good clean healthy substance is critical to reaching a high level of performance.

During my lifetime of personal experiences and study of my own life, as well as those who I have met and counseled, I have learned that your thoughts, what you believe, and the confidence you have in yourself, are the key to your eventual success!

The more I worked with top competitors, in sports and in other fields of endeavors, including business, careers of all types, as well as those just trying to be able to deal with their daily individual struggles, then the more I realized the importance of first and foremost feeding the mind with positive, encouraging, inspiring and empowering thoughts. This is the foundation necessary to carry the physical or tangible part of our lives to any winning situation.

In my first published book *Face Fear Create Courage* I discussed in individual chapters the importance of concepts of "The Power of Thought", "The Power of Words", as well as the laws of Oriental wisdom known as Yin and Yang. This last concept relates how everything in nature and the universe is comprised of seemingly opposing forces that constantly work together and are actually interconnected to create the necessary flow of life. This includes the balance and harmony we need to overcome our challenges.

I give an example that I share immediately with everyone I train, counsel or work with, about how our minds can trump the physical. It is relatively easy for us to walk a two or three foot wide board that is placed on the ground. We can lean, stick out a leg or our arms out over the edge of it with little or no effort. But yet the same board placed fifty feet in the air becomes an obstacle of overwhelming proportion. Thoughts have an incredible power over everything we experience in life.

Our thoughts and minds are the way we relate to, interpret and create the successes and failures in our lives. No matter the size, strength or quality of our physical body or any tangible material at our disposal, our minds ability to create, control and use it to the nth power will determine our final result.

This fact has led me to always consider the importance of supplying the mind with clean, positive, nourishing substances or "mind food" just as I would always try to do the same for my physical self in order to have at my disposal and command an efficient tool to use in order to create success in whatever the goal. This is what led to the birth of my second book, *Power Thoughts – Motivational Fuel for Success*, and this the second - Power Thoughts – The Gift Of Adversity.

The interesting and strange thing is that all the Power Thoughts that I share and have written in my blog and in this book, I also read to help remind me and empower me in my walk through life. Although I wrote them, they do not come from me. Instead they come through me from a Universal Intelligence that is in every living thing on this planet and part of all of us. We all have access to it, if we only slow down and shut out the constant clatter that our lives produce in our minds. I hope you enjoy and can efficiently find a way to use it in whatever your goal may be.

There are a lot of programs and books that try to help you with the subject of motivation, but they only cover one or two areas of what you need to really get yourself going. Until now!

"Power thoughts" addresses, first and foremost, the most important aspect that will help you with whatever your particular and personal issues may be. Your perspective and foundation of how you deal with your life's experiences! It then goes on, with hundreds of power thoughts, how this principle applies to the myriad of different scenarios that we will all eventually face in one way or another.

This is why I have collected and put together these Power Thoughts that I know will help you on your journey to achieving your biggest goals and your chosen destination!!

To really appreciate and understand the layout of what will be in the quotes, I feel I should start with what has been taught in the East for thousands of years and that has helped me to understand fully every subject I have ventured to learn. As you will see, it is at the base of everything in the universe. As I previously mentioned it was an important chapter in my first publication *Face Fear Create Courage* as well as in *Power Thoughts Motivational Fuel for Success*. I feel it will be beneficial to you as you absorb each of these power thoughts to use this most profound and ancient Eastern wisdom. Enjoy.

CHAPTER ONE

The Dynamics of Yin and Yang

In every disaster, there lies the seed of a potential benefit.

This section of the book contains the groundwork to help you develop a clearer and more proficient game plan for your life—one that can help you understand reality, the universal laws of physics, their relation to the human body and mind, and your interaction with the world around you.

To truly grasp these principles and the fundamental concepts that support them, we need go no further than the laws and the teachings that have permeated Asian culture known as the yin and yang.

This symbol is associated with the majority of martial arts styles and Eastern culture. It originated thousands of years ago and is a profound way of seeing the way nature exists. It is at the foundation of everything we see. It is at the root of mathematics, because without "nothingness," what exists cannot be. Binary arithmetic, based on one and zero, has made computers possible. The principles of yin and yang are more apparent in our lives than we can imagine. They represent the perpetual balance that exists in the universe and our lives. We need to understand their meaning and tap into the power they use effortlessly. Nature exists in perfect balance, for everything it takes away, it gives you something in return. Balance and harmony are the foundations of wisdom.

Whenever I begin a class, I ask students, including some that have studied Asian cultures, philosophies, and the concept of yin and yang, if they are familiar with this symbol. They typically answer with "It stands for hard and soft" or "It stands for male and female." Although these answers are correct, they are only a small part of its complexity.

It is a symbol that represents an idea that everything we know is governed by the underlying truth that all things are made up of seemingly opposite positive and negative energies that continuously blend together in harmony with one another. Everything in the universe is affected in some way by this principle of opposites blending harmoniously.

The art of life is not seen as holding to yang and banishing yin but as keeping the two in balance, because there cannot be one without the other. This is right; this is wrong. I like this; I don't like that. According to Buddhist beliefs, these dualities are the source of suffering and problems. Dividing up our world in this way is false thinking. Things do not either exist or not exist; they do both. All computations were revolutionized by the recognition that "nothing" was "something." It is the law of perpetuity that makes our continued existence possible.

The Harmony of Opposites

Notice that day turns into night and night to day as does summer and winter, life and death, as well as all things in nature. Opposites blend by becoming each other or being a part of each other, thus the dot of black in the white and the dot of white in the black that we see in the yin and yang symbol illustrated.

In other words, when it's daytime, we seek the shade. When it's nighttime, we turn on the lights. When it's hot, we look for cool. When it's cold, we seek the warmth. When it rains, we wait for sunny days. When it's dry, we pray for rain. When we're young, we want to be older. And when we get old, we want to be younger, and so on and so on.

They are not just harmoniously blending constantly with each other, but also continuously exist within one another. We should accept and appreciate this and that all things need to be in harmony in order to continue the smooth cycle of life. To make it easier to understand this, here is a partial list of simple examples in different categories. See if you can add some more to this list.

Day	Night
Sun	Moon
Summer	Winter
Spring	Fall
Hot	Cold
Soft	Hard
Rough	Smooth
In	Out
Up	Down
Left	Right
Relaxed	Tense
Tall	Short
Addition	Subtraction
Division	Multiplication
Action	Reaction
Straight	Circular
Light	Dark
Inhale	Exhale
Rich	Poor
Loud	Quiet
Full	Empty
Happiness	Sadness
Love	Hate
Pain	Pleasure
Mind	Body
Debits	Credits
Laughing	Crying
Cowardice	Courage
Health	Sickness
Strength	Weakness

These things endlessly permeate our existence and thoughts. I share with my students that these are all, individually, things we know, and yet we never put them together.

Everything is different, but everything is the same in some way. The human body as we have already mentioned is mental and physical and these need to be in harmony. We can all know what it takes to lose weight, to quit smoking, to stop an addiction. But knowing, and doing, are two different things. Knowing is only half the equation. The mind and body must become one in order to accomplish our goals.

Regardless of the subject, to be able to comprehend it better, we need to reduce it to the most common denominator or establish a sense of relation or comparison to it. This can be seen as a way to see the complexity of our universe in its simplest terms.

As you read this book, your mind absorbs it as chapters, pages, paragraphs, sentences, words, and letters, dots, and commas, and yet at the same time, you reverse the process to ingest the information.

In mathematics, we look for common denominators to solve equations; in chemistry, we see matter as molecules, molecules to atoms, atoms to protons and neutrons. Recently, DNA has further increased our understanding of ourselves. In war, if you can divide your enemy into separate groups, they will be easier to conquer.

You can deal with problems and fears in the same way, one day at a time, by breaking them into parts and by taking on the small ones first. All the Power Thoughts in some way will refer to this phenomenon throughout this study. Keep this in mind and it will help you better understand the different subjects in each of the quotes. Note that, although these ideas can be easier to recognize and grasp when they are more tangible as strategy applied to visible physical encounters, they are just as readily effective with any verbal or mental conflict.

There are numerous examples throughout these chapters. Look for them. Study them and the ways you can apply them to yourself. The Bible is about good and evil. The book of Ecclesiastes, which was authored by King Solomon, a man whom God blessed with the gift of great wisdom, states this:

There is a time for everything and a season for every activity under heaven. A time to be born and a time to die, A time to plant and time to uproot,

A time to kill and a time to heal, A time to tear down and a time to build, A time to weep and a time to laugh, A time to mourn and a time to dance, A time to scatter stones and a time to gather them, A time to embrace and a time to refrain, A time to keep and a time to throw away, A time to tear and a time to mend, A time to speak and a time to be silent, A time to love and a time to hate, A time for war and a time for peace.

After facing so many instances where I tried to make things happen the way I wanted, this passage helped me to learn one of the greatest lessons in my life and brought a glorious calm over me. Although you may try, you cannot always control the things that happen to you or the world around you. The one thing you can control is how your mind perceives things and your ability to see them as both positive and negative so that you can better adapt. You must appreciate your strengths and your weaknesses. Learn to accept life, and do your best to blend with it. However good or bad a situation is, it is both, and it will also change.

Let's continue this train of thought to see more of this law of yin and yang. Our brain has two sides. One side (left) absorbs and interprets words, numbers, the linear, and so on—basic logical things. The other side (right), interprets pictures, color, concepts—emotional, intuitive, creative, and spiritual things.

Electricity has negative and positive poles, as do magnets that we find in the earth. When we move, one muscle tightens and contracts while the opposing one relaxes and stretches. When our eye sees, it sees exact vision as well as peripheral vision. When we breathe, we inhale oxygen and exhale poisonous carbon dioxide, and yet the trees and plants around us take in the carbon dioxide and give us back pure oxygen. This is the harmony found in nature.

It's interesting to note that you can't start your car if the battery cable is connected to only the positive. You also have to connect the negative cable. Life is constantly yin and yang. We must learn to take the good along with the bad. The master understands the death of a caterpillar is the birth of a butterfly. Be the master in your life.

A most important maxim is "There is no disaster that can't become a blessing, and no blessing that can't become a disaster." People refer to karma as destiny, but in fact, the word actually translates as "action and reaction."

Traditional Buddhist law of dependent origination holds that every cause has an effect and that every effect has a cause.

As you accept these facts, you can appreciate that any situation—physical, mental, or emotional—is subject to the yin and yang. Just as we realize that we cannot control either side, we understand that we need to embrace who and where we are by accepting the situation and blending with it. Problems and fear will overwhelm you when you fight them. But they can also be beneficial and a necessary ally. By accepting the situation you can become one with it and get through it. We will discuss how to use and appreciate life's and use them to your advantage. As you walk the two-by-four of life, focus on walking it and not on the fear of falling or failing. Be in the moment.

The more you understand and are in harmony with your own mind and body, the more you can be in harmony with those around you. This is not necessarily to control, but to better understand how to adapt to the situation or better appreciate or accept the circumstance. To be in harmony with yourself as well as those around you is the first step to conquering any obstacle. The foundation to inner peace and true enlightenment is to accept that everyone and everything is interdependent. You must emotionalize and practice these concepts.

This balance we all need relates to your life in numerous ways. From the need to balance your budget to balancing your emotions, you must consider two sides to every decision. In the following chapters, you will find how this balance applies to all types of situations and how you can flow with life's many challenges by blending with, and not fighting, the circumstances you will encounter. Now that you are becoming more familiar with the yin and yang principles, let's discuss how they apply to you, your life, and the choices you make.

Important Bullet Points

1. Realize that there are two sides to every story.
2. Try to see the yin and yang in all things so as to not make one-sided choices.

3.   Be your own devil's advocate or seek out another point of view.

4.   Accept the situation you are in as both good and bad, and see how you can blend it.

5.   Realize your struggle or fear is both big and small and good and bad, depending what you are comparing it to and how you approach it.

6.   You are the way you see yourself. You are in control of your point of view.

7.   There are things you don't have that someone else has, but there are things you have that someone else lacks.

8.   The water that can take you to the bottom and drown you is the same water you need to swim to the top.

9.   Be proactive. Don't wait to fall in the water before you learn how to swim.

10.   Balance the opposites that affect your life. This is important.

11.   Realize that Everything difficult is also simple once you accept and understand it.

12.   By improving yourself, you help others, and by helping others, you improve yourself.

13.   Break down your fears and problems to help you overcome them.

14.   Everything is different and the same. Use what you know to help you understand what you don't know.

15.   Realize that Your pain, suffering, and obstacles will benefit you or may be to help others. We are all interdependent.

16.   Tap into your strengths as well as your weaknesses, as they both serve a purpose.

17.   The good or bad of any situation you face depends on your perspective, and your perspective depends on you.

18.   Failure and pain are a necessary part of your successes and pleasures.

19.   Everything in your life is as important as it is insignificant.

20.   Be in the moment.

CHAPTER TWO

POWER THOUGHTS

1. That's the Truth

   The principles of yin and yang prevail over all creation. Everything is continuously made up of opposites that are intertwined so they are not really opposites but part of the one and of each other.

   There is no absolute truth. Events, people, politics, religion are viewed and become different realities or truths only in the minds of different people depending on their perspective. We each create our own reality that is the world we live in. All truth can be untruth and untruth can be truth.

2. The Secret to Success

It is not the one with the most money, strength, speed or potential who wins the day. It is the person who blends, adopts and uses everything available to them, including the challenge itself. In every success, you see there is no one specific thing you could pin-point, name and sell as the secret to that success.

There needs to be a harmony and interaction between the integral parts of any object or circumstance that makes it what it is and gives it its true power.

Being in the "Zone", or in Zen being at one with the universe or the things around us, joins us together with nature and the laws that give it power. In sports, business, or in any situation or in life, taking advantage of what is available is the key to victory.

3. Change Yourself

When wanting someone to improve their life the way you feel would benefit them, be sure that your intentions are not really to benefit yourself. Let them be who they choose to be. Either they change or they don't change, but you can change your perception of them by acquiring the ability to accept and to be at peace with who they choose to be, even if it means having to break ties with them!

4. Accept Failure

Between you and success, there are failures you'll have to endure. No one knows the exact number, so your probability of success increases by failing as many times as you can. Never be afraid of failure. It's what you will find on the road your dreams and desires.

5.   Zen proverb.

The obstacle is the path.

6. Live and Learn

    Knowledge is acquired by memorization and recall of information, circumstances and events. Wisdom is achieved through struggle, hardships and unpleasant experiences.

7. Lying for Compassion

How many times do you not answer someone's question truthfully and honestly because you don't want to hurt their feelings, insult or anger them? How often do you make yourself miserable because you don't speak up in situations you need to confront but are "afraid" to face?

Your reasoning of being kind, caring or compassionate to others or just fear makes you not only insincere as you lie your way out of saying what's truthfully in your heart, or just to avoid confrontation. But then, others will see you as someone you are not, since they see and judge you by how you tell them you think and by what you say and do! You are giving them misinformation, and their view of you and your character is based on a lie.

How many times do people offer, promise or state that they are going to do something and then don't show or come up with the stupidest excuses of why they didn't follow through? The worst is when they hear you could use a favor and offer themselves and won't take no for an answer. The feeling of generosity and benevolence and immediate gratification they feel and are trying to make you feel is not only worthless, but a disrespectful action when they break their word.

When you speak honestly and from your heart, you give people the gift of the beauty of relating to the real "you". A friendship, relation or conversation of any kind cannot become a reality, thrive or last long, if it is based on lies or does not represent the real you and the truths you are committed to!! Your concern of how anyone will misinterpret what you say is irrelevant. If you don't like something someone said, or they ask you "your honest opinion" don't tell them what you think they want to hear, speak what you feel in your mind and heart. Do yourself and others a favor and base your relations on truthfulness.

8. Generosity

    Fear makes us cling tightly to what we have. But what you give comes back to you. It is an investment that will pay high dividends. Be generous with your time friendship, hugs, compliments, love, and praise.

    Happiness and wealth don't always go together, but happiness and a generous spirit are almost inseparable! Amazing joy, freedom, and fulfillment come when we choose to live with a generous spirit.

9. Doubt

    Doubt is not always a negative thing. Don't doubt that you can succeed or doubt that it will happen. Instead doubt that you can't or that it won't happen! Everything can be negative or positive.

10. Be In the Moment

A person who can conquer fear, will find peace and calm in their heart, remain composed and, be content wherever they find themselves. That person is the one who will enjoy the scenery regardless where they are or when they must take a detour to get where they need to be.

11. A Higher Level

We have within us the capability to connect with a higher self, a super conscious state of mind. We can become one with a universal and divine intelligence that can help us see some of the experiences and circumstances we have from a totally and more profound perspective and insight.

We must learn all about ourselves, mentally, physically, emotionally and spiritually, but our daily activities and details keep us from achieving this. The more time we spend alone, in introspection, the clearer this becomes to us. The Greek philosopher Polonius said "This above all: to thine own self be true, And it must follow, as the night the day, Thou canst not then be false to any man."

12. Your True Depth

Once you accept the laws of nature and the yin and yang of life, you will see that you are like a lake or pool of water. It could be clear and clean on the surface yet dirty and mucky on the bottom. Whatever happens on the surface, whatever storms or choppy circumstances cause disturbances, just like the ocean, do not affect the bottom or depths of your whole being or the total of who you are.

13. It is what it is

As I look back on the total of my life, I have discovered how often our constant obsession with all the things that we want and desire, keeps us from recognizing and appraising the value of all the truly meaningful things we already possess. Our mad quest for who we are so desperately trying to become in our lives, keeps us from seeing and appreciating the total worth of who we truly are.

14. Stop Procrastinating

You will achieve your goals and dreams when you begin to take action to pursue them with determination, commitment and courage. Use the power of the great force found in the dynamics of yin and yang, nature and in the words that state "As you sow, so shall you reap."

15. Appreciate Life

It would be an impossibility to never encounter what, at first, may seem like a stressful, negative situation or circumstance in our lives. But if we can always remember and consider that the laws of negative and positive exist in everything there is, then we will see that they are opposite sides of the same coin.

Your ability to flip the coin and see exactly how what is happening can be beneficial to you. It will give you a totally new perspective that you can use to appreciate, be grateful for and constantly flow in a happy and contented life, no matter what comes your way.

16. Knock, Knock

Opportunity doesn't knock often but doubt is constantly banging on the door.

17. What Do We Really Know?

Our ability to learn is a most important human trait. We will never reach the point where we know everything we need to learn about what we are supposed to know.

The need to review, relearn or keep up with the constant advancements in everything we think we know is a survival skill we can't do without.

18. Master Your Ignorance

The term "master" is a misnomer. It has as much worth as it is worthless. I would rather be called Master Wu - Shih (nothing special). Zen teaches you to do your best always. That I will always do. You could live a thousand years and not know everything there is to know about any one subject. To think that you are, or anyone else is, a "Master" in martial arts or even a master craftsmen is to admit you are a fool. We never stop learning.

We must never stop learning. Doctors, surgeons and other professionals, all have continuing education plans and goals. Part of their résumé is their ongoing education. Professional accreditation requires such plans.

I am on a quest to master myself. To get as close to enlightenment as my years will permit me. To be enlightened means to understand the yin and yang of life. Do not judge yourself. Do not feel sorry for yourself; do not be proud of yourself. You are not one side or another of any title, you are both.

Neither love yourself, nor hate yourself. There is no "me" or "I" there is no longer a relationship with you but one that you have with the universe. There is no "self" to defend or protect anymore. Loving and knowing me will be the main focus of all my relationships. This is not an easy task, but life itself isn't either.

19. Your Magical Genie

We are all in possession of the proverbial Genie in a bottle that can grant you every wish and desire you can dream of.

Your life is the bottle and your thoughts are the Genie.

If you present to your Genie skepticism, fear, anger, laziness, hatred, sadness, jealousy, contempt, illness, greed, lack, self-pity and lack of forgiveness to others, he will grant you all these things.

If you speak to your genie of hope, courage, commitment, love, compassion, trust, forgiveness, dedication, health, caring, giving and goodness he will bring these out of your bottle and give you more happiness and contentment than you could ever dream possible.

20. What Are We Doing Here

We are in a constant mental battle. Our ego is afraid of its own death or losing to circumstances, arguments or situations. Our pride, and the fear of failure, loss or being wrong is where we feel threatened and what confronts us each day.

Our ego and our need to be right is the real opponent. This is why we fight with friends, in relationships and wars are being fought around the world this very moment.

Accepting the reality that we are nothing more than fools playing a game we don't understand all the rules to, and know even less about its final purpose, it will release us from the pressures and worry of being right or wrong, and will in turn let us deal more intelligently with others, the outside world and the obstacles we must face daily.

21. Enjoy the Flight

A mother bird will hunt for worms, come back to the nest, chew them up and regurgitate them into the wide open mouth of her baby chicks. As they grow she will just come back throw the worm in the nest and let them feed themselves.

Eventually she pushes them out of the nest for them to go out, fly on their own, hunt and fend for themselves. We as humans also go through a similar process.

Some of us become addicted to not having any responsibilities, being fed, would rather remain in the nest, wait, have to fight for our share of regurgitated food, grow weak and be nothing more than an easy target for predators.

Grow up, learn to fly, explore the world, beautiful skies, and enjoy all the delicacies that are available to you.

22. Connect with the Force

    Meditation and prayer are the best and only way we have
    to connect with peace, love, harmony, the universal essence,
    wisdom and The Force we are all part of and can use in
    dealing with daily life.

23. Every Day Meditation

Zen meditation teaches us to be in the Now, a way of focusing or being in the zone. Great artist, athletes, musicians, craftsmen and others, achieve this state of mind when performing. You can use this to improve your own performance in whatever you choose.

You can practice this next time you are doing any routine activity like brushing your teeth, washing your hands, walking up or down stairs or anything else. Observe every movement, the sound of the water, your breathing, your every intricate movement. Pay attention to all your senses. Notice the feeling of calm and concentrated focus you begin to achieve.

Become aware of your sense of presence. You will feel yourself getting better at it. Then try it next time you're doing something that requires your full attention, calmness, concentration and full mind body synchronization. When you're losing your cool in traffic, work, or any other frustrating situation, breath, stay calm. Life can be a joyful adventure.

24. What Is Your Why?

The why of your purpose gives you the fuel to never give up, to persevere and not obsess about the when, your why will help you figure out your how so you can reach the where you want to be.

25. You Never Know

Sometimes the only way to go is to set what may seem like unrealistic goals and just go for them buoyed on ignorance and enthusiasm! You can do all sorts of things when you don't know you can't do them.

26. Cherish the Moment

Your goals are not destinations that you must desperately worry about reaching or accomplishing. They are a process, journeys that are for you to enjoy. Succeeding or failing is irrelevant.

You should live every minute of them with anticipation, wonder, and appreciation for the opportunity to be on the personalized and unique adventures of life that you have been given or chosen for yourself.

27. Feel It

What you think is not as important as what you feel. It's your emotions that inspire your thoughts into reality.

28. Easy Does It

   Most of us have a tendency to shy away from things if they seem risky or difficult. We have a natural response that makes us not want to take risk or struggle, mentally or physically, with any task we take on. We like things to be easy with guarantees. We don't like the uncomfortable thoughts of doubt, fear, or possibility of failure we associate with it. But risk and struggle are an integral part of any achievement. By embracing them, you embrace success.

29. Taking Action

We may clearly know and understand what is the right thing for us to do, the road we need to follow, the things we need to accomplish our goal or our purpose. But our thoughts without the harmony and unity with the physical and tangible are meaningless. We must take action in order to complete the cycle needed to create them into reality.

Whether our goals are to improve our health, finances, knowledge, relationship, or anything else, we will reach them by taking one step or one small action at a time. Anywhere you are going to go is done one day, one step at a time. Take the first step today!

30. Wisdom

We're always searching for the answers we need in our lives from somewhere or someone else. No one and nowhere else can you find the real answers to your most important questions. Like the ones that tell you when you're in love, when you're happy, or when you're feeling sad, or depressed.

We are so influenced and controlled by the noise of the world and the people around us that we don't listen to or sometimes just ignore when the truth and the only voice we can really trust speak to us.

Take the time to appreciate being alone with your thoughts and connecting to the intuitive and divine intelligence that is your true guide.

31. Invisible Power

As much as it is doubted and criticized, the power of meditation, prayer, or likewise harmonious connection between a person's mind, spirit, and body, can have a profound and strength giving effect on them, another individual, or a collective group.

In 1998 at Duke University, a team through valid scientific experiments verified that prayer, does indeed, albeit a mystery, have power. 150 patients who had undergone invasive cardiac procedures were studied. They were divided into two groups, none of them knew they were being prayed for. 7 religious groups around the world were asked to pray for them. The researchers took into account all manners of variables including blood pressure, heart rate, and clinical outcomes.

The prayed for group seemed to recover much better. The minds intentioned to make them better had an effect across the space-time, boundary. Prayer is a quantum event that is carried out through invisible mind power vibrations and energy. Science, which seems to be the most credible modern religion, through these controlled experiments, made it clearly evident that this mysterious energy and force does exist.

32. Creatively Clever

Whenever we are confronted by an intricate or difficult problem, in life, business, at work or with any circumstance, the ability to make the best move when there are no good moves available, to renegotiate with reality with a strong yet calm State of Mind can mean the difference between success or failure.

This entails the ability to be creatively clever and come up with a new idea that will just pop into your head, like the proverbial light bulb, when you deliberately try to find something good in a bad situation.

Apply the law of Ying and Yang and remember that the solution is always hidden within the problem.

33. Detachment

When a family member, friend or neighbor is facing an emotional challenge we know deep inside the perfect words and advice to give them, and when we are having the same problem, they would probably know to give us the same exact advice that at that moment we can't see.

The reason is we are not as emotionally attached. Do you realize you know better than anyone how to deal with your own problems, you just don't trust or listen to your inner voice enough to follow your own advice and wisdom?

34. Why Do Certain Things Happen

We all have probably heard, used, or have had to face and accept the truth in the expression that goes "Everything happens for a reason."

The conundrum lies in the fact that we must accept that we lack the insight when the incident is occurring or the foresight to know why. Only with time and ability to appreciate that there is a hidden value can we continue the forward movement, flow and progress that we need in our lives.

35. The Real You

Ten different people have ten different perspectives of you and who they expect you to be to them. Be yourself -you can't please everybody - they won't all always agree with the many sides of your personality anyway.

36. Subconscious Learning

We all instinctively or through osmosis study copy, emulate or follow the example of others. This can be good if you're mentors or people you admire are of good character and positive guides. But in can be detrimental if those you look up to or emulate are highly dysfunctional.

Be careful and selective about those you surround yourself with and learn from. We become most like the closest five people we associate with. This could be the difference between great achievements or disastrous failures.

37. Our Interaction

Since childhood and as we grow older we realize the need to look up to and learn from people with more time on this earth, knowledge or experience with any given subject. We are also helping others in the same way.

No matter how old or how much ability or knowledge we acquire, we will still live under the same circumstances.

Every Champion needs a coach.

We will always need someone to help motivate, Inspire, and empower us to be the best that we can be as well as pass on what we can to others. I hope that our relationship gives me the opportunity to share what I can with you as well as get feedback from all of you so I can continue to grow and learn more about what I have chosen as my life's purpose.

38. An Evil Within

Regardless of our gender, education, or position in life we all have inside us a demon that is capable of the most heinous and savage actions. Most of us are taught from an early age by our parents and society to be kind, benevolent and caring to others. The majority of us spend the rest of our lives trying to quash this inherent evil that resides deep within our thoughts and be the loving and caring individuals we have been programmed to be. But life provides us with struggle.

For some, due in part to the consequences that are part of these struggles as well as the need to experience the egos defense mode of hate, anger and survival that influence our thoughts, are not able to conquer the pressure created by the feelings that burn and boil inside. They explode in ways that go beyond the scope of what would be acceptable in a civilized society.

For others love, kindness, submission to circumstances, and fear keep them in check. One or the other of these two powerful combinations of forces will win.

We judge and criticize others as they confront and react to their own battle. Whether we accept or deny this conundrum we are all bound by it and will face its reality sooner or later.

39. Who Changes

Sometimes in a personal, business or work relationship with someone, you realize that the other person is not willing to change their attitude or perspective. When you stop trying to change others and work on changing yourself or the situation your world changes for the better.

40. "What da they got that I ain't got?"

"In The Wizard of Oz, we remember the Cowardly Lion when he is describing courageous situations and asks, "What do they got that I ain't got?" In unison, the rest of the group says, "Courage." Yet not until he went on his quest with the group and he was given the medal by the wizard to affirm his courageous deeds did he lift his chest in total confidence.

In the famous lyrics from the song "Tin Man" by the group America, it says, "Oz never did give nothing to the Tin Man that he didn't already have." We all possess the ability to have courage in the face of danger.

Courage is defined in the dictionary as "the ability to face difficulty or danger with firmness and without fear." In fact, it is not the lack of fear but the presence of it that triggers courage and bravery. One cannot exist without the other.

Courage is a necessary and integral part of success in any endeavor. We all seek and need encouragement. Parents, coaches, teachers, friends, people, or ideals that help us face our challenges with boldness are greatly treasured. Courage is a virtue that we all need on a daily basis.

Courage will not always be synonymous with heroic action. Courage will be present in our character regardless of the consequences of our actions. At times, we will need courage to persevere in spite of failure. Whatever the circumstance, we must find the courage to face both large and small challenges.

The willingness to sacrifice whatever is asked of us—even to the death—can give us superhuman capabilities and the strength to conquer our dreams and desires.

President Obama said, of police officers, "They run toward the danger, not away from it," he said during a White House ceremony for award-winning police officers from across the country.

The passengers on Flight 93 overcame terrorists and crashed their plane rather than permit them to fly the plane into another building, perhaps the US Capitol.

"Greater love hath no man than this, that a man lay down his life for his friends."
John 15:13

41. Watch Your Step

What to everyone including yourself, may seem like a lucky break or an unfortunate situation occurring in your life is actually the results and outcome of traveling on a road you've been on for a while. Our Life is comprised of a long journey that we are taking one step at a time, day by day.

No matter what the original destination may have been, every turn, every step can potentially change the direction in which we're heading and can make a dramatic difference to where we end up. Be wary, vigilant and constantly review your map and original plans so that you don't get distracted and lose your way.

42. Teamwork

It's amazing what you can accomplish as a group if you don't care who gets the credit.

43. Rough Roads

It is not probable that you will reach or achieve every goal that you strive and work hard towards. That's fine. It's the process that will be beneficial to you. It's the obstacles and failures you will overcome that will help build the discipline, attitude, and character that will ultimately help you succeed and end up where you're supposed to be.

It is not a smooth carefree road to success and goals. Your plans should not be so specific as to not have wiggle room. Realize that circumstances in life that you have no control over will affect the journey to your specific goal. Be pliable and able to adjust to whatever unexpected obstacles you may confront or need to deal with on your way to your final destination.

Strive for success as an individual of commitment, strength, and character and your goal will be at the end of whatever road you must take.

44. Enjoy Life's Competition

Every aspect of my life, as with everyone else's will be exposed and subjected to failures and successes. From the beginning to the end you will forced to confront battles you must fight.

The wonderful thing about it is that when you choose to be a warrior, a fighter, and it's what you enjoy and strive for, It makes life exciting, adventurous, and worth living.

Nothing is worse than not living life to the fullest and instead having to experience a dull, mundane, uneventful existence.

45. Average or Totally Unique

The concept of average is used in anything from clothing, seats, and everything imaginable. It necessitated the term of "adjustable" because like the law of yin and yang dictates, everything, including humans, are all the same but yet different.

You and your life are also both; you should constantly strive to be the special individual that you feel in your heart. You can be average height, weight or anything else but your thoughts are really what distinguish you from everyone else. You are unique, one of a kind. Don't let yourself succumb to everyone's idea of how you should adjust to their idea of who or what you should be.

46. Sharing

Sometimes, we keep from giving or sharing what we have with others because we feel a sense of lack in our own lives. We do this with material things as well as spiritually when we fail to give someone a compliment, a kind word, support, love or forgiveness. We are all not weak or have needs in the same spots. You will find that by helping someone fill their need, they can in turn help you fill yours.

47. Someday

   Never wait for "someday," some other time, or a special occasion to do something with or say something to someone. Everyday can be that "someday" or be the perfect day to start your quest. You may never get another chance.

48. Trade Karmas

By improving yourself, you can help others, and by helping others you will improve yourself.

49. Being Judgmental or racist

Throughout history, certain people, ethnic groups and races have established and distinguished themselves with customs, attributes or some expertise or lack thereof or by their circumstances and how they dealt with them and developed as a people. In nature every living creature lives alongside of and interacts with every other species, sometimes in peace and harmony and sometimes with violence and yet still in harmony. Every race has both poor and wealthy representatives that are worthless excuses for human beings and every race has those that make you proud to be whatever you are.

As far as your association with these "other" people or anyone you meet, either you can be naive, overly trusting and continue the same course or you can start to be more careful and let people individually prove themselves as being sincere, a decent person and citizens of the world before you tag them with a generalization, or judge them as white black, Spanish, Asian or other.

The yin yang of life dictates that we are all different but yet the same. You say Spanish people are loud, talk fast, argue with each other and you can't understand them when they get together ...you are right. But that can be said about Italians, Irish, blacks or Asians or any race. Now you must accept the good and the bad about your ethnicity. If something that is said about your ethnicity or a group you associate with and it bothers you then maybe you should work at helping your "FAMILY" get ahead, improve their mindset, perspective and situation so they can rise above the negative side of their customs, behavior, how they are seen or being identified.

We all have both good and bad in ourselves, our families and our ethnic backgrounds. Suck it up!! You, your family, your race, they all have good and bad points. Accept that and try to improve yourself as well as those around you rather than defending something that has no excuse, reason or reasonable, fair or just defense.

But remember "Birds of a feather flock together" so be particular about who you associate yourself with.

50. Life's Gift

The energy, force, power, and the presence of a universal and divine intelligence surrounds us and always available to us. Use it wisely.

51. Develop Real Power

It's a natural human trait to strive to be stronger individuals. We all consciously or unconsciously crave and want power. We also don't like to feel others have power over us. We want to overpower the competition, or adversaries of any kind, be it in conversations or other encounters in life. We want to feel like we're in control, be winners not losers.

Sometimes we fail to realize how internal power trumps the physical, over ourselves as well as others. This translates into a feeling that turns our daily existence into a constant struggle, with our minds as well as with family, friends and strangers. We try to execute our power with situations or in our roles as leaders, parents, employers or in relationships.

We usually associate power with material things like money, shelter, food, clothing and other objects. We come to realize internal and emotional power and also try using this by controlling or restricting favors, compliments, friendship, love, forgiveness or even conversation. We don't want to relinquish our power. We often feel that by empowering others we give them power over us. The truth is that the more you empower others the more powerful you become. Giving yourself or others one minute to lift the spirit is worth more than years of denying it because of ego, resentment, revenge or guilt. Measure your personal power not by how much you have over others, but how much you have over yourself. Don't keep yourself from developing real power.

52. How's Business, How's Life?

I've been speaking with friends who have started or know someone that has a business and it's not going well. As I ask questions I realize that there's one common denominator. Regardless of the business that you're in or what your product is the first and foremost thing you're selling enthusiasm, smiles, and conversation. No one likes to go to a place where they don't feel welcomed or pick up on positive motivating vibrations.

Your mood will reflect all accompanying interaction. When you feel comfortable or happy with someone or a place, you will tend to engage more with whatever you're doing. In business you have a tendency to buy more or at least look around and see if you can pick out something you like, especially if the rep is engaging, cordial and gregarious. Look at any successful business and you'll find this quality present.

It's the same with your life. Be sure that you or your employees are enthusiastic, smiling and selling themselves first, your product or service will follow suit

53. Experience

There is a learning tool I refer to and explain in the book *Power Thoughts – Motivational Fuel for Success*, called "The Ten Steps to Success". I have used it in lectures, teaching any subject from business, to fighting to preparing a party or event.

The steps follow a sequential pattern of most to least important but they all depend, compliment and are in harmony with each other. Knowledge or understanding is number one with any subject and yet is totally useless without number three which is Experience.

No amount of accumulative knowledge, understanding or perceived insight of anything can be fully reached without experiencing it. Some things can only be known through experiencing them. Don't let the fact that you may not totally comprehend something keep you from trying or experiencing life. Doing is part of learning, and learning is part of success.

54. Your Personal Growth

These power thoughts are not meant to sell or give you magic beans. They contain within them motivation, inspiration and other principals that you must extract that will empower you to nurture and stay on your path of personal growth.

55. Thoughts Create Your Destiny

Just like our mind can make our muscles tense up and relax to move us in different ways physically, it also affects our physical being by making us have energy, feel weak, motivated depressed or a number of other states including our health. Your thoughts can create your day to be a wonderful day or a calamity. The human body is built to adjust, repair or adapt itself to whatever attacks it which include negative thoughts.

56. Don't Be Dissuaded

When pursuing your goal, don't be discouraged by new obstacles along the way. Opposing forces rise in proportion to the size of your challenge. There is nothing that doesn't adjust and balance itself to maintain the flow of its existence.

57. The Answer You Seek

Every new idea, invention or solution came about by combining or rearranging what was already known. We seldom totally understand or appreciate the answer to our dilemma because we often fail to see or we ignore the obvious. The Answer is found by studying the problem.

58. Internal Battles

Some of us feel we are not fighters, competitors or like confrontation. I always ask people, "When was the last time you got into a fight"? They stare into space trying to recall an incident. That's because we immediately think physical, but we fight daily with our own thoughts, compete against circumstances and struggle when we confront adversities. We need to use the way of harmony, the only approach that gives us the ability to blend, flow, truly understand and be in tune with the obstacles and challenges that we face daily and the greatest and most powerful opponent that you'll ever meet, yourself!

59. Learn Control

We need to work with both our physical and mental, as well as our spiritual aspects in order to deal with the world around us. From a physical perspective, the better you can control your feet, hands, timing, range, coordination, strength, and speed, the better you will be able to understand and deal with and control someone else's.

Likewise, the more you can understand and control your mind and different emotions, the better you will be able to understand and deal and blend with the circumstances, events and people around you. Remember your mind is where the control panel that connects to everything physical and tangible. In this way, you can gain greater control of your life.

60. Save Yourself

The waters that can take you to the bottom and drown you are the same waters that you need to swim to the top!

61. Strengths and Weaknesses

Be aware and tap into your strengths as well as your weaknesses, they are both have a useful purpose to you.

62. Enjoy Who and Where You Are

We are all preoccupied with the fear of growing old, death and the unknown. When we're young we want to be old but when we get old we want to be young. We obsess with ways to fight it, with what we wear, make-up, surgery, exercise, mid-life crisis, potions, always trying feel and look younger. We fail to be in the moment and enjoy the value of every day and every minute and often miss the real purpose and beauty of ourselves and our lives.

63. The Power of Knowledge

We have an instinctive tendency to fear what we don't understand. Do your best to understand more and strive to acquire new knowledge. Knowledge creates courage. Courage creates opportunities. Opportunities create successes. Successes create advancements.

64. A Powerful Force

Our increased knowledge in quantum physics has revealed to us that we and everything around us is fundamentally electric energy and vibrations.

Things, even what we may consider as an inanimate object also possess, transmit as well as receive this energy. A gift or artifact projects an energy that you can sense, mentally, physically, and emotionally. Your demeanor as well as the clothing you wear emanates energy or vibrations that others can pick up. We sometimes use it simplistically or superficially to judge others by, but psychics who practice and deliberately tune in to it can pick up more from a piece of clothing or objects that have absorbed this energy, sometimes even to help solve crimes.

You too are made of this energy and force. You are very special and have amazing gift and abilities beyond your wildest imagination. Don't let yourself be afraid, feel weak, helpless or inadequate in any way. Have the courage to seek out and discover your strengths, the opportunities, adventures and marvelous things that we all dreamed of and imagined conquering as children. You are and can do more than you ever thought possible.

65. Creating Character

You are daily creating your character. It is the foundation of who you are and who you will be in the future. You are doing it by what or who you listen to, what you say, what you experience, what you do; what inspires you, what moves you mentally and spiritually, what you have a passion for, and the philosophy you live by. These are the building blocks of character that will lead you to greatness.

66. Adjust and Make It Happen

Sometimes we have to make adjustments to aim for our goal or purpose. Few of us are willing to make radical changes in our lives. Fate is how your life unfolds when you let fear or doubt determine your choices or say, "let's see what happens."

The destiny you can create will be when you confront your fears and make a conscious choice to make something happen, to commit, adjust and hit your target. Take the necessary steps to make the best of a bad situation; this will empower you to reach your goal.

67. Plan

It is crucial to the success of anything we do, to plan and put everything in order. We must organize, align, adjust and arrange our plans based on reality, actual truths and principles. More importantly we must accept and be at one with the fact that there is already, in place, a flow and Divine Order to the universe and everything in it.

68. Struggles

Your struggles, troubles, the experiences and the philosophy you use to overcome them will help you gain strength and confidence to face the challenges in your life. Through this you will encourage and empower others. Stay focused on your purpose and not your problems. Always Face your Fears, you will Create Courage.

69. The Strongest Drug

In the book *Face Fear Create Courage,* I made reference to how, even with fear, familiarity breeds contempt. What we really become immune to, like any other drug after constant use, is the adrenaline and endorphins cocktail rush that at first we mistakenly judge as fear.

After all the wild and crazy adventures I have survived, I just don't react to the rush like I used to. At first my youth's testosterone pumped body and my mind's lust for an action-packed life was absorbing It like chugging down a beer. As you grow older and the more you shoot it into your veins the more your mind detaches itself from the physical body or event to a point where it almost becomes boring. That's when you must focus on it to give you strength and a feeling of immunity to doubt, pain or the fear of failure.

You can also experience this when you have a strong willed sense of purpose. It happens to fighters, athletes, performers and anyone whose desire to conquer the moment supersedes the overwhelming fears and doubts of any obstacle or challenge before them. We all have this ability. We just have to tap into it and let it flow. It is the greatest high you could ever imagine. The feeling of not letting yourself lose control of your emotions is true mastery!

The hardest of your emotions to control totally will be the drug called love, but it too can be defeated. The last part of overcoming your relationship with it will be the love you have for this dream you are experiencing called life. Death will be the last fear you will need to conquer. Then you will have reached the final and highest level of your journey through this time and space. To achieve this use, live, and enjoy every day like it's your last.

70. A Real Champion

Anyone can run a sprint. Some can run miles. But only a champion will go the distance when the length of the race is unknown.

71. It's All You

We think that our thoughts, our circumstances and how we behave are caused by how we are treated by others and things that happen to us in our lives. It's actually the reverse! The events we experience and the interactions we have with others are a direct and exact reflection of our actions and consistent thoughts. We create what we experience and how people treat us. We are quick to take credit and shower ourselves with accolades for all the good things that happen to us, but immediately look at what or who we can point fingers at when disaster or bad situations arise in our lives. We must realize that we retain a lot of our childish ways and habits we acquired as we were growing up and creating who we would be as "adults".

We all need to work at growth and make daily improvements. If you live 100 years, you will hopefully still be learning and growing, both intellectually and emotionally. Stop trying to find blame or cause outside of yourselves and take responsibility for who you are and for each and everything you face in your life. Through your responses and actions you have created the person you are today.

72. Choices and Decisions

Life is a constant road of what often may be tough choices and decisions. Making them can be stressful and consuming. You must find within you the courage to take a leap of faith-- even when the consequences may seem vague or unknown.

Fear and doubt will keep you in a frozen catatonic state. By not making a decision and bravely accepting responsibility for whatever the outcome, you will guarantee certain failure of the circumstance or of character. Most importantly, you will never discover what might have been! Live life to the fullest or die trying.

73. Outside Your Comfort Zone

We all think that if we think positive that it is going make us feel good. And that's not true. You can say to yourself, I'm going to improve my situation, I'm going to start my own business, I want to make more money. I want to get in shape. I want to win a championship, I want a better job. I want to write a book or any number of things that would seem like a positive move in your life but all these things are going to take work. They are going to make you have to step out of your comfort zone.

We are creatures of habit, which means change hurts. To accomplish things you're going to have to make mistakes, experience failures, come up with new ideas, take chances. All these things don't always feel so good. They make us uncomfortable, that is why so many of us settle for where we are and get in a rut with our lives. When you accept the yin and yang of life, that things will bring you both joy and pain, that's when you will find happiness. You will also find contentment and empowerment in having courageously taken the journey into an adventurous unknown.

74. A Poem about Life

"They'll always be change that appears in your life, some brings contentment, and some will bring strife.

Some will be happy some will be sad, some will be good and some will be bad.

And then there's the one thing that you can control, and that's how you take things and then how you roll.

So keep a good attitude stored deep in your mind and you will see treasures in all that you find."

75. Overwhelmed?

If we saw in one lump sum, the amount of money we will need in the next year for food, gas, rent, or other expenses to simply survive we would have a panic attack. An ant cannot leap across the yard but he can advance inch by inch. Fear, doubt and worry are the unnecessary interest we pay on the problems we see tomorrow.

76. Dream Big

We are all dreamers, but to be a successful dreamer, you must possess this one quality, to have a profound and real commitment to pursuing your goal. You have an incredible power within you that can overcome any limitations. You must have the courage to take chances, to be determined and dedicated to the journey towards your destiny to dream big.

77. Recharge Yourself

In these hectic and busy times, we are constantly surrounded by people and busy with situations that are sometimes beyond our control. We all need a little push, a pat on the back, or just a little encouragement. But even when someone tries their best to cheer you on or say something they feel will help you move forward, it seems it's of little help.

This is the moment that can be of benefit to you if you realize that you, for all intents and purposes, are basically alone in this big world.

It can be the perfect time you need to just connect with yourself and go to that special place that encourages, motivates, empowers, and gives you the boost you need to carry on. No one else has a greater connection to the universal essence, force and power that is all around us than you. You need this solitude and alone time to be able to tap into it mentally, emotionally, and spiritually.

78. Equal Exchange

You acquire your greatest value and strengths from your worst experiences.

79. Be Prepared

If you expect to succeed to overcome and achieve a goal, be prepared to fight for it. If you expect to fight be prepared to commit. If you're willing to commit be prepared to give 100% and never give up. This means being prepared to do whatever needs to be done. If you're willing to do whatever needs to be done. You must also be prepared for whatever the outcome and accept the consequences. Any doubt or fear you may feel at first is just a thought. You will perform and achieve exactly what you believe and are prepared for.

80. A Mantra for Life

I will not leave this earth without first living out the adventure that I envisioned my life to be. I have never and will never live in fear of failure or doubt of the challenges I may face or of what I know I am capable of being. I intend to use every day to the fullest. I will not cower to whatever obstacles stand in my way.

I will find a way to conquer and complete every goal my mind conjures. I will not burnout my remaining years slowly like a candle but fly to my greatest heights like an invincible dragon, burst into flames and come down in a fiery blaze of glory and reappear like the legendary phoenix.

81. Your #1 Goal

In competition of any kind, as well as in life, you have numerous goals you will want or need to attain. To come out ahead, to succeed, to follow your game plan, to use one technique or another, to achieve a personal best, to avoid injury, the list can be diverse and endless. As important as all these points may be, trying to focus on too many goals can keep you from accomplishing any of them.

The one key to conquering any and all activities you take on is to keep an inner calm and composed mind. This should be your number one goal and the one thing that will bring forth all the physical strengths, training, and preparations you have been working on for achieving any goal. Don't let a cluttered or scattered mind stop you in your tracks.

82. Your Ego is mistaken

In an insane way to protect itself, our ego conditions our mind to hate being wrong. We try avoiding it at all cost to the point of it being detrimental to our own efforts. Fear and doubt are strong emotions that bully the trust and confidence we have in ourselves. These doubts and fears will predict failure on the basis that our quest and goals may appear too difficult and we are bound to fail.

Our ego's inherent need to feel good about being "right" about our predictions overrides the feeling of being wrong about our doubts and fears. We subconsciously throw a wrench into our efforts. As crazy as this may sound, this is how our thoughts that should be working in our favor end up working against us and thwart our chances of success. Your ego can be your worst enemy.

83. The Power of Meditation.

You naturally possess an ability that is used by you and others to influence your actions more often than you realize. Self-hypnosis can be achieved unconsciously and influence you in positive as well as negative ways. Hypnosis is a form of meditation that can be achieved by helping you to focus on specific thoughts and word patterns. A hypnotist helps you tap into your own ability to relax and focus to a very intense level. Meditation is practiced in countless ways. Each country, each religion has its own means of meditation for spiritual discipline, healing practice, or a way of experiencing psychological growth. We engage in meditation, because it can be empowering, healing, rewarding, and peaceful. Research into the use of the power of thought, and meditation, has shown it to be effective in reducing pain and useful with simple illnesses as well as with chronic diseases.

Meditation is a process that can help you focus your thoughts on the immediacy and feelings associated with any action. You can build up the strength of your mind and your awareness. This can help you develop a form of self-hypnosis that will empower you when performing any task.

We need to recognize that prayer, as controversial as it may seem, can be considered not only a way of communicating with God but also as a form of meditation or concentration that can have some powerful results. The word "inspire" breaks down to being "in spirit."

Successful people work at meditating and developing positive thoughts and good habits. Champions repeat an action until it becomes second nature so they can duplicate it under pressure. They practice both mentally and physically. Doing it mentally (visualizing it) is as important as doing it physically.

Research conducted at American University followed three hundred students, half of which practiced meditation on a daily basis over a three-month period. Subjects in the meditation group considerably lowered their psychological distress levels while strengthening their coping ability.

84. Pride

Pride is a beneficial and common human trait to strive to be outstanding, different, and or noticed. But this, when not in balance, can sometimes bring out the worst in a person and with it grief and suffering.

85. Believe in yourself!

When I was a child, each time I faced adversity and survived a dangerous or frightful situation, it made me think that I was somehow special, protected, perhaps here for some greater purpose. Whether or not that was the case never really mattered. But my believing it gave me the courage to seek adventure and take chances, some that didn't seem like the best way to go.

The philosophy of yin yang teaches you how and why there needs to be harmony between the ups and downs that occur in your life. This harmony as well as the necessary interaction between you and the events and situations with the rest of the world is what make you who you are. This harmony and interaction is part of life. The more you can see this, the more you will be able to flow and find peace.

The most important way that I have been able to use and appreciate the philosophy of yin and yang in life is when people say to me, "You're so lucky. Everything seems to work out for you." Actually, by applying the principle that every situation can be both good and bad, I look at how whatever is happening, even when it seems bad, can be good for me, and I use that as the stepping stone to move forward.

Being aware of our inner capabilities can help us meet life's situations calmly and more energetically. This can be the basis for developing a Zen-like approach when dealing with fear and the choices you face. If your mind is clear and aware, you will find it easier to focus on what you are doing.

Now I consider myself, as is taught in the Chan principle of Zen, wu-shih ("nothing special"), yet I approach any challenge with the confidence that I will use whatever happens to help me succeed. All of us, at the same time, are dumb and smart, strong and weak, good looking or not, or any other opposites. The difference comes from to whom or to what you compare yourself.

86. Your Title Fight

After coaching so many athletes for their particular challenge, goal or world title, I use the analogy when counseling or working with others in different areas, that we are all in constant preparation for our own struggle or world class fight. Our fight to succeed, to better ourselves, sometimes it's a fight to just get out of bed in the morning. We are in a fight to conquer and win over daily problems with our finances, relationships, as parents, students, life partners, or just to be happy.

We are inside the ring called life. By ourselves, alone, no one but us and the opposition, We have to remember our training, our commitment, our goal, our purpose, the big prize. We must draw on our courage, our passion, our do or die attitude to succeed. We need to control our emotions and cannot let fear, doubt pain or struggle to overtake our biggest strength, and that is the will to win! That is what I tell them, what the voice in your corner, your trainer, your biggest ally and fan, your own mind, needs to tell you. And you must listen! Be the champion you know you can be.

87. True Wealth

We equate being rich with financial abundance and being poor with the adverse, a lack of cash flow or material possessions. But these actually take a back seat on your journey of what is truly valuable in your life. Being poor is a state of mind that can also relate to poor health, having poor verbal skills, education, poor social skills, and the one thing that can be the cause of the scarcity of all these which is poor self-image or self-esteem.

When it comes to true riches, it would probably be more important to consider having valuable friendships, good health, truly loving relationship with family, or that special someone, or being happy with ourselves and who we are as our real wealth. It is said that no one calls for their banker or accountant when on their death bed. What do you consider when calculating your wealth and valuable assets?

88. Acceptance

Do you want to be totally fearless? Never, ever be afraid again, of anything? Here's how. If you want to overcome any fear you have of doing anything you want, whether it's to compete in any sport, get on stage, say something to someone, take on a new challenge, start a new business, quit a job, be alone, move to a new place, of falling in love, conquering any goal or anything else, the way to do it is to accept the feeling that comes with it. This is the yin and yang of every situation. That's what you're afraid of. It's not succeeding or the event you're afraid of, it's the feeling or emotional sensation that comes along with it if you fail, the hurt, the pain, the disappointment. And that is an unavoidable part of the equation.

Fighting is a good analogy. Everybody thinks a fighter is not afraid to fight, or get up in the ring, or get hit, or that it doesn't hurt. He is afraid, it does hurt him to get hit, and like any other performer, he worries about looking bad, or losing. The big difference is that his desire to win, to succeed, to feel the rush of being on top, to overcome the challenge, is greater than the pain or anything else that may come with it. Being totally at one with and accepting the inevitable two sides, the negative as well as the positive, makes you the master of your life. Being willing to die makes you enjoy and love life. Cowards die a thousand deaths, heroes only once.

89. Life's Journey

I am trying to see where I am, with no real idea
where I'll be.
But must trust in a plan that's much larger than me
I know when I get there my heart will say "WOW"
And I realize how much I need to grow now.
Cause all that is outside and bigger than me.
Is just the reflection I nurture to be.

90. Stone or Dust

You will enjoy happy thoughts and spend wonderful moments with family and friends, chisel them in stone, lock them up and preserve them in your heart. You will also have irritating thoughts and share aggravating moments with them, throw those up like dust into the wind and let them fly far away from your mind.

91. Slip Sliding Away

Simon and Garfunkel had a hit song back in the 70s called "Slip-Sliding Away". The lyrics said, 'You know the nearer your destination the more you slip sliding away'. I love this song; it speaks the greatest of truths. This is the story of our lives. By the time we learn the lessons we need and are fulfilling our dreams and goals, our lives are well on their way, and the time we have to enjoy our achievements is almost over. Cherish and celebrate and enjoy every day, every moment, every failure, every success and everyone that shared them with you as well. They are the most wonderful part of the journey you are on.

92. Don't get wound Up

We all inevitably discover that we possess a kink in our armor or some flaw in our physical, mental, or emotional self. This fact can sometimes consume us as we try to become the ideal version of who we think we are or desire to be. We need to accept that our negatives as well as our positive traits are part of what makes us human.

As we direct our attention on, and try to correct or fix a presumed flaw, it can grow in our minds to a point of obsession and actually direct our path to that end. Instead, try focusing your intent on discovering and nurturing the most beneficial qualities that make up the total of who you are.

93. The Real Truth?

Throughout our lives, we are exposed to "bits of wisdom" that may sound profound but are not necessarily true. In one of my previous posts, I remarked about the saying "Seeing is believing" and how that's not true. You have to believe something before you can see it or it becomes a reality. Every great invention and everything we see around us was a thought that someone believed in and made it happen.

There is another bit of wisdom that we've all heard, "Treat others as you would have them treat you." This is also not entirely true. We are all different and have different likes and dislikes. In any interaction with another person or to have and maintain an honest and beneficial relationship to both parties, you should treat them as they deserve to be treated. It's not about you and what you wish, like or would want for them. It's about what that person creates, attracts and draws into their own life from you, others or from the universe.

94. Emotional Power

Your emotions have power because you will think what you feel. Your thoughts have power because your thoughts become a belief. Your beliefs have the power to attract and become your reality. You are and will become your emotional state of being. How are you feeling today?

95. Your Torch

We are all sparks, embers or flames in a big fire of energy that comprises the Universe!! We will all eventually die out. But our purpose in life is to help that fire and force shine bright and grow in a positive and forward movement. This is the true purpose of life! The yin and yang of life is clear. We are all interdependent.

The more you help another individual, their spark or flame to ignite and burn with their potential, the higher your own, as well as the energy of the Force that we are all part of will shine. Help encourage, motivate, inspire and lift another individual in their goals and watch how it will come back and reward the same to you!

96. A Battle Within

The fear of failure or criticism can be more powerful and exhausting than the desire to steadfastly walk the road to success. But don't you give up!

97. Growth

We are an active, constantly growing process. We are meant to improve and to become better than we are at any given moment, time, or place in our lives. Never give up striving to be a greater version of yourself than you were yesterday.

98. What Will It Take?

Sometimes it takes a life-altering encounter or experience to get you on the course you need to follow.

99. A Leap into the Unknown

As kids, most might remember gumball machines and the surprise prize, it was a big plastic ball for 25 cents. You didn't know what you were getting, usually something not worth more than a few pennies, but you took a chance and spent your hard earned money on the chance it just might turn out to be something valuable.

As we grow older, we lose that thrill of jumping into something that may or not may not pay off. Actually, the gimmick is still out there, it's called the lottery. You take the plunge and throw your money at something that the chances of winning anything are very doubtful.

We may not play the lottery, but we still play the same game in life. There's an addicting thrill in taking a blind chance and leaping into the unknown that makes life an exciting adventure. A feeling that lets you relive being a kid again and having that youth filled spirit of conquering and succeeding at the unknown. When was the last time you took that leap?

100. Creating Castles

At times, it will seem like it's taking forever for things to happen or for you to complete your project. But it's not forever. Your life, in relation to time, is over in the blink of an eye. Each minute, each hour, each day that goes by is a precious gift. These days are the building blocks you will use to construct the castles that are your dreams and aspirations.

The consistency with which we use each of our days to create what we strive for and desire is important. They are scarce! The longer you put off your goals, the less chance you have of ever achieving them. Every day you let slip by, like misplaced bricks without mortar, will turn to dust.

I have had the opportunity to participate in and attend marathons where thousands of people start, and before the first mile, hundreds find some excuse not to continue. How many people apply to colleges, and how many follow through and graduate? How many types of businesses open every day, and how many make it past the first year?

Of course, you can always find an excuse and call it "a good reason." Many of us praise and give ourselves the credit when things go right but blame our misfortunes or failures on someone or something else.

The truth is, somewhere during the process, we didn't use enough building blocks or tossed them haphazardly at dreams to see if we might get a chance hit. Or we hope that our building blocks might fall into the right place. Don't count on it. These blocks which represent commitment, consistency, and effort must be handled with great care.

They must be put in the right place so that we never have to regret how or why they were used. Most of us have had the time to lay the foundations for our castles. How strong is yours?

You still have time. Stay on that road. Walk it often. Stick with it. Maintain the commitment to your goals, your work, your friends, your family, your business, and your life.

Believe in and tap into the supernatural powers that we all possess. Discover how you can enjoy the happiness and fulfillment that creating your destiny will bring.

101. Focus on Your Intent

To allow thoughts of worry or doubt to appear in your mind when jumping from one spot to another, or going from one moment in your life to the next, is like grabbing on to an anchor. Your mind should be totally occupied with either jumping or landing. Be in the now, and go with the flow of the energy you are producing. A bird in flight does not stop to wonder how it flies or what would happen if it fell to the ground. Nor does a gazelle stop to think about what it feels like to be eaten by a lion.

102. Reality or Fantasy

The imagination can create unbelievable fantasies. This can be good when writing fiction, making a movie, or telling a story. But it can be very detrimental when we fail to see the difference or start to believe the fantasy of what we say and the reality of what we are willing to do.

There is a difference between the fantasy or promise when receiving a college degree, and the reality of creating a successful career, of falling in love, and the reality of a day to day relationship or marriage, of training in the boxing gym, and the reality of fighting in the ring in front of a crowd for a world title, and the fantasy between getting a black belt in a karate school, and having a real life or death street fight.

The difference is in the courage of your mind and body to be willing to sacrifice everything in order to reach your goal. Anyone can talk a big game, that's the fantasy. The reality is the willingness to back it up when the time of reckoning comes. Words can create the fantasy; your actions create the reality. Be real!

103. While You Still Can

Your life in relation to time is over in a blink of an eye, in milliseconds. Take advantage of the short amount of time you have on this Earth to appreciate it, and enjoy it with yourself, your loved ones and with your friends. Don't be shy or timid. Have the courage to give it your best shot. Have the courage to take chances, to express you mentally, physically and verbally any and every opportunity you get.

Consider that you may not be here tomorrow, and be candid, be truthful and forthcoming with the way you act, feel and think. Take this opportunity to tell those that you care for, those that have meant something to you in your life that you appreciate and love them. Tell those that you might feel you neglected or let down, that you apologize and are sorry, tell those that you know who belittled, maligned, and tried to hold you back that, although you know their intentions weren't to serve your best interest, that you're not fooled and yet still appreciate them.

If, when you're gone, you have the opportunity to look back, be sure that you never regret having left something undone, onset, or not having used every second you were allotted.

104. Life's Reflections

The laws of nature, duality and their continuous harmony dictate that what you teach, is what you are learning. What you project reflects back and projects on you. Life mirrors what you put in front of it.

Although we try to deny responsibility for the chaos in our lives, what we plant is what we will grow and consume.

Everything I have accomplished, acquired and experienced as well as everything I have failed at, lost and suffered through were a product of my thoughts and daily behavior. Whatever you create in your mind, think of consistently, hold true to in your heart and your actions will manifest themselves in your life. Be aware and cautious even of what you may sometimes unconsciously project.

105. Real Friends

Finding true friends in life is like searching for gold or diamonds; you will have to dig through tons of dirt and rock to find one truly valuable diamond or one pure ounce of gold. Finding one is not the end. Smoothing out the rough spots, or cutting a diamond, is the process of heightening the friendship. Finding one is a beginning.

106. Weapon or Tool

Love can be a powerful tool. It can be used to construct strong, meaningful, joy filled lasting friendships and relationships. But it can also be also be a weapon that can control and destroy self-esteem, self-worth, and self-pride. It can be both used by you as well as used against you.

When used positively, it can be beneficial by building up, encouraging, inspiring, and motivating the human Spirit to its highest level. When used in a negative way, it can cut through someone like a razor in the form of initiating a feeling of rejection, guilt, pity, helplessness, depression and potential loss.

It is an internal, emotional and non-physical way that is used by many to control situations as well as others. It is a power that can trump any knife, gun, ropes or chains to keep someone in a frozen catatonic state that can keep them from moving forward and confined to an invisible prison of pain and suffering.

The good news is that we each individually hold the key that can help us break free and fly away to the joy of life we know we deserve.

107. Self-Control

Today's society is plagued with drugs, alcohol, crime, a weakness and behavior that is destroying our country. It's not any one particular drug, substance, or food that is the biggest culprit in the deterioration of the quality of our lives, it is self-abuse brought on by the lack of discipline.

We have become a generation of finger pointing, excuse oriented people. It's always someone or something else's fault. We can find dozens of reasons for whatever befalls us other than taking personal responsibility. We, each of us individually and collectively, are responsible for the life we live.

The minute you take responsibility for You, yourself, you will be empowered. It will be the moment you are no longer a slave to circumstances.

108. Real Gold

In whatever you may choose as a goal, the measure of your achieving success or considering yourself as having arrived, of being a true warrior and worth more than any prize, accolades, money, degree of "winning" or "title," is dependent on one simple thing.

For martial artist, any athlete, a business person, musician, artist, a fighter, or anything else, the willingness to face whatever doubts, fears, obstacles, setbacks, losses, pain, suffering, being knocked out, losing, even if it takes death to achieve, is where you will find the real gold.

There is no greater feeling, no greater rush or high, nothing can taste better than having conquered yourself. To jump off that cliff into the abyss of the unknown is what the throngs of people at any event cheer and crave for but will never possess. That is the difference between being just a dreamer, a wannabe, just part of the audience, or considering yourself a winner in life, really means.

109. Eye Focus

Your eyes have the capacity to hold focus and show intent. When you speak to someone you are sending energy, with your eyes you combine attention with intention. Focusing in on someone's eyes as they speak to you can tell you more about what they're saying then their words can.

110. Dying Ain't Much Of A Living

When it's your turn to die, no one can die your death for you. Likewise appreciate that and the fact that today is your turn to live, and no one but you can live your life for you! Are you feeling lucky?

111. You will find everything you need

From childhood to your senior years, your talents, abilities and potential are not set in stone. Every day of your life you are in a process of growth, evolving and becoming. Once you set your course and intent the Universe will work alongside of you and provide the opportunities to get what you will need. You can overcome what may seem like insurmountable challenges.

Don't let yourself become complacent, discouraged or let yourself give up because you don't see everything you need placed neatly in front of you. Enjoy the challenges. It's not that you won't have it; it will appear when you need it.

112. Or Die Trying

Death is your greatest Challenger. The best and most formidable opponent you will ever encounter. The one you can learn the most from. It challenges you to live, to appreciate the moment, the people and the opportunities that you have before you. It will inspire you to take advantage of the now. To do your best to reach your highest level, to overcome any obstacle you may face.

The majority of us try our best to shy away from it, we ignore it, and we make believe it's not there. But it's always there patiently waiting for us to acknowledge it, to accept the fact that sooner or later our time will run out and we will have to face it. You can cower and hide, or confront it fearlessly and courageously.

To really live life, to achieve and overcome any goal or challenge, whatever that may be, you have to sacrifice yourself. You must give it every ounce of blood sweat and tears you have in you in order to reach your goal. You must be willing to give it everything you've got. There is no greater failure in life than the failure to not go for it, do your ultimate best or die trying.

113. Enjoying Your Meditation

When I'm doing a sculpture, (my interpretation of Moses in Black stone) a painting, working out, or any other activity, it is a form of Zen meditation. A way of calming my mind, getting inside myself and tapping into the collective consciousness, the Creative Energy and God force that is inside of all of us. People often tell me they can't paint, draw, or sculpture.

Any activity combined with your creative abilities can be a form of meditation. It could be cooking, music, arranging your furniture, writing a letter, cleaning the house, raising a family, work or any task you may be facing. You see it in your mind; you become one with your project and you methodically and efficiently transform it into a reality. This is what you can call being in the zone.

You do it to the best of your ability, not for anyone else's Judgment of how well or bad you did. You do it just for the sake of doing a good job. It is the best way to tap into your physical, mental, and spiritual self. You will enjoy being in the now just for the sake of being, of doing, of living and experiencing the moment to the fullest.

114. Expectations

Our expectations of ourselves, of what others think of us, or of life, can be a source of great suffering. Expectations relate to who we ourselves or others think we should be. This can become stressful because of our inability to fully see or accept who we are in total. It can also be difficult to understand because we are a combination of many things. These include all of our emotions, our titles, our careers and of course who we in our own minds think we are at any given moment.

We add to the confusion by judging ourselves by what we have or haven't done, or by our possessions of what we have or don't have. Any of which taken separately are meaningless because they do not give a clear and accurate description of the total of who we are. Accepting this dichotomy will bring relief because until the day we die, we are in a state of becoming.

115. Inspiration and Enthusiasm

Enthusiasm fuels inspiration. The word enthusiasm derives from the Greek word 'entheos' a God or spirit within. Webster defines inspiration as: to encourage, move, or guide by Divine or Supernatural influence. When combined, these are the most potent formula for success and achievement with any goal. Tap into the force and energy of the universal spirit that is within you and part of every living thing.

116. The Wonder of You

Take a moment to look around and see how Mother Nature proudly displays its wondrous beauty and perfection. It's almost like it gives extra care and help to the flowers, plants, trees, and all living things that struggle the hardest to survive. As human being, you are one of its Nature's greatest creations. The more effort you put into growing, flourishing, and expanding as an individual, the more that the energy, force and power that is in all of creation will work within you.

Appreciate, respect, and utilize your body, your mind, your talents and the amazing creature that you are as an individual!

117. Creating You

The energy that your mind and thoughts project, and the energy that your emotions and Heart project must be joined together in a focused harmonious stream in order for their force and power to be turned into the tangible and physical reality that is you. The walk you walk must be as strong as the talk you talk. Knowing and believing is only the first half of doing and achieving!

118. Thoughts Become Reality.

I strongly believe and always advocate the power of thought and visualization to create new circumstances or conditions; this will help you with your plans and goals, in training your athletic physical abilities or anything tangible in your life.

You need to see it in your mind's eye before you can make it a reality. There has been extensive research that supports the idea of how linking visualization tremendously improves motivation, confidence and performance or the quality of the final action or product.

119. I KNOW WHAT I'M DOING!

I know what I'm doing!! Everyone has heard that phrase. From kids, co-workers, friends or even shout it out there yourself a couple of times.

The truth is you could live a thousand years and not "know" everything there is to know about just one subject!

The next thing to consider is that knowing and the ability to perform a task first well, then very good, then flawlessly and then instinctively are totally different things!! That is why every athletes and champions need coaches and trainers. Why boxers need corner men.

Your ability to take in, rationalize, plan out strategy, and or execute the action is seen from two perspectives. I referred to this on the post about emotions. The person in the middle of the mix, action, competition, performance or struggle, the person on the outside, regardless of their relation, concern or own desires are not as "emotionally attached" and see things that you too would see if you were watching yourself.

We all may know what to do but sometimes we forget.

120. The Hidden Power

We all have to conclude and accept the fact that there is energy, a force, a power that is part of us as well as part of everything in the universe and in every living organism in this world. Whatever term you want to use to call it, be it the Universal Intelligence, Mother Nature, The Force, God, or even if you want to deny it exists, It exists!

I just read a book that I found to be very profound and revealing by Mark Twain. He lays out an interesting premise in his work, 'Letters from Earth'. When the Archangels were trying to decide where the great force that is God should hide, they decided against suggestions like the moon, deep beneath the surface of the sea and others. They concluded that man would sooner or later figure it out. They decided to hide him within every human being because 'the last place man would ever search for him is within himself'.

The same Force and energy that creates all things and keeps things constantly flowing is within us all. We can choose to connect to it, use it to grow, improve, and help ourselves and others rise to the highest level of our potential, and manifest miraculous things in our lives or we can ignore it, deny it, and just waste this opportunity we have been given in life.

121. The Weed That Is Fear

There is nothing that is immune from fear. From something you may have to face, be nurturing, need to do, to something you may not want to lose or be without, can all be choked and killed by this destructive and yet sometimes seemingly harmless emotion.

Your mind is the soil in which it will use to sprout and develop, your doubts and negative thoughts are its seeds, what it will feed on and need to grow, right alongside your prized plants and beautiful flowers.

Pull it out by the roots! Don't let it destroy the beauty you can create and enjoy in the garden that is your life.

122. Judgments

Pointing fingers, condemnation, blaming others for our personal mistakes, errors in judgment as well as guilt, will disappear with self-awareness and self- acceptance. All judgments will reveal themselves to be self - judgments. When we choose to accept and understand this, our capacity to appreciate ourselves and the true nature of life increases.

123. Emotions Committee

Imagine that all your different emotions like fear, doubt, love, greed, pride, courage and the rest were each individually represented by one member of a committee that advises and counsels you but inevitably has a strong say in controlling the decisions and direction you take in your life.

Each member gets one vote when making decisions. Each member has the opportunity and is committed to make the case for its emotion. But you, as final judge must also listen to and weigh each members arguments. In these decision making meetings there will be debates but the final vote must be cast by each member and must consider above all your progress and growth. Your goal is to make the final decision and final choice of which direction to take based on a balanced look at each situation and by a mutual vote.

No one emotion can force or control a decision. When that happens, your emotion of hate, love, greed, compassion, lust, pity, fear or any of the rest will lead you into making a constant flow of regrettable decisions.

124. Knowledge in Action

Knowledge is useless without personal effort, creativity and ingenuity being applied to turn it into an applicable reality.

125. Emotions and Character

Our emotions, and the way we respond to them, create what is often called 'character. It is character that will determine success or failure and character is always a work in progress.

126. Going Up

You can get to the top of the most attractive and highest ladder you could choose and discover it was taking you to the wrong place?

127. Your Emotions Create You!

Are you totally content with who you are, what you do, where you live, your job, who you're with? We relate to our physical reality via our senses. As complicated as your life may seem, it was always under two main categories, pain and pleasure.

As toddlers, we didn't seem to like or care much for pain, but as we grew older, we found out that every time we faced and endured something that hurt, it made us stronger. You made all sorts of choices and decisions along the way. All of these moments and the road you take are influenced by your different emotions.

It's always easy for you to coach someone, or else tell a friend, family member or acquaintance what they need to do in their lives or with their problem or situation, and nine out of ten times you're probably right. The simple reason is that, no matter how much you care for that person, you don't share the same emotional attachment to the problem they are facing or the need to face the situation yourself.

We all share and have the same emotions both nurtured and genetic. How you confront, deal with and use them is where we differ and where you have control. This can help make you a winner or a loser!! It's up to you.

As an artist, the more you understand the color, texture, shades of your paints, the different strokes, brushes and how they can be used on a canvas, the more beautiful and satisfying your final masterpiece will be. Likewise when painting the blank canvas that is life. Be aware how often your knee-jerk immediate or uncontrolled emotional response makes you think, say, do something or put you in a position you later regret.

Strengthening your ability to deal with the minds response to the emotions associated with your experiences is the only way to carry your life to peace and contentment!

128. See and Listen

We are given the opportunity, and may have the capability to look at and hear the truth, but it only benefits those who choose consciously to see and listen.

129. Who Are You?

Your ego can keep you living the fantasy of thinking you are the person that you imagine yourself to be, and wish that you could be, rather than the reality of who you really are.

130. Are you Winning or Losing

Your confusion about the answer starts with the misconception that you are in competition with others. You're not! The yin yang of life dictates that you will always be a loser because there will always be someone who, on any given day, will beat you. You will always be a winner because from day one of whatever your endeavor, there will be someone you can crush.

YOU are your number one adversary and the person who you must challenge and defeat on a daily basis. You can use others to gauge your progress or lack thereof, but that's it.

Remember, it's not just training and strengthening your physical abilities; it's strengthening and developing your character that counts.

The people that let their ego control who they are trying to become, will never reach their most valuable goal, self-improvement.

Others will ultimately see you for how hard you tried and how far you progressed, not what you did or didn't accomplish. The fact you failed the first few times should serve as a drum roll of tense anticipation to the climax of your achievement.

131. Discord

Ego and pride are the biggest deterrents to settling or reconciling disagreements or differences between acquaintances, friends, or relationships.

132. Using what you don't have.

We would all love to have everything fall into place with the plans we make, but sometimes life happens! You must use your creative abilities and have the passion to accomplish your goal, but you must learn to take advantage of what you don't have. What you don't have, need or want, is the foundation of what you will achieve! The principles of yin yang use what you can't do to help you accomplish what you want.

I have had the opportunity to learn, not only from how I have turned my own inadequacies and failures into successes, but also from helping others plan out solutions by using the ability to see the yin yang or opposite energy in all things that keeps the world going round.

The ability to accept what isn't available, whatever happens, including failure in spite of all our efforts, is the catalyst that puts our mind in a position where its potential can be multiplied to unimaginable heights.

133. Spiritual Strength

In a previous power of thought, I referred to the fact that the old adage that says 'seeing is believing' is incorrect. We feel that, what our physical eyes can't see, does not exist. Actually, we must first believe something in order to bring it to fruition. This has been proven by every great inventor and explorer who believed in something that everyone else doubted and ridiculed him for even thinking.

Remember that the word "inspire" is comprised of two words that refer to being "in- spirit." Don't let naysayers and doubters keep you from expressing your spiritual and heartfelt beliefs in the Force that you are part. This can keep you from using this inherent strength to create real substance and happiness in your life.

134. Young at Heart

The majority of your achievements and accomplishments were made when you were young, bold, a dreamer, impulsive, brash, arrogant, a risk taker and a know-it-all, Don't let time, age or previous failures let yourself become discouraged or complacent and keep you from going even further or reaching new goals. Live and enjoy life till the very end.

135. Resentment or Contentment

Happiness is built on a foundation of contentment. Wherever you find yourself, even if you feel lost and tired, appreciate that you are at a place where you have an opportunity to recoup, adjust and discover new found strength.

136. You have to Learn Success

I had the good fortune to meet and learn from mentors who taught me the principles of success. To have the courage to take chances, be committed, respect yourself and others, being creative, and working smart. I soon became a success. Unfortunately, my wild adventurous spirit and fearless love of danger got me involved in a criminal lifestyle where money, guns, new cars, and a wild life were the marks of success.

This can be a difficult and unforgiving road to travel. It took me inevitably to a gangster's life of greed, deceit, treachery, guns, illegal activities and the lowest possible place a human being can find himself, a world of drug dealing, alcohol and drug addiction, prison, being shot by the police, being on the run for years, homelessness and the need to be scraping the bottom of the barrel.

Once I decided to leave that lifestyle behind and play the game in the legal world, I made millions and lost it all a number of times. But once you have practiced and used the principles of success, they will work for you over and over again! Life can be a beautiful adventure, but you must learn the game of success and apply it sincerely and diligently to your career, family, business, or whatever area you choose, so you can take it to the top and live it to the fullest.

137. Right or Wrong

As important as it is to have purpose, a cause, or a definite position to drive us, the worst thing we can do is to hang on stubbornly to an idea or become a blind follower of one point of view, a particular thing or of anyone or anything, to the point of being a hard head or fanatic. Be it in an argument, politics, religion, philosophy, or ideology, always keep an open mind!

Don't let your emotions cloud your rational judgment. The law of Duality, that is an unavoidable part of all things, makes possible the fact we can be as wrong as we are right.

Nothing is permanent; everything is in a constant flow of change. Keep an open mind and leave yourself some wiggle room, or you might find yourself bound and tied up in a position of looking totally foolish and ignorant with no way to escape or place to go!

138. Lost Opportunities

It is amazing how we as humans fail to appreciate or care for what we have immediately available to us in life. No one gave great concern about Clint Eastwood, Charles Bronson, Bruce Lee, Michael Angelo, Marco Polo, Christopher Columbus or even Jesus in their own land or home. They had to leave for other places before they found people that saw their worth. When you die, people cry, send flowers, and speak of what a great person you were but while you were alive they didn't call, care if you needed help, were sad, broke or in trouble.

Don't let this happen to you. Be grateful for the people in your life. Show them you care, love them, call them, help them when need be. Someday they will be gone. And it will be too late. Don't bother showing up for my funeral... Those that know me know that every so often I will call you if I have your number. Not to ask for something, but to see how you are feeling or if you need something. My friends on Facebook, I comment or like some of the silly or even personal stuff they post. I have hundreds of "friends" and only have a few that remark or seem to notice the comments or advise that I share. That's what friends do. Now that I am traveling promoting my book and meeting new people, I have found they see me in a totally different light than those to whom I gave my time, commitment, knowledge and anything else I possessed, including my life.

If you die tomorrow and have a moment to look back, you will wish you would have told that friend or person you loved them, know that you supported them in whatever way they needed, that you appreciated a favor, or perhaps to let them know that you thought they were being unfair, cheating you, or treating you unjustly. Take the time to acknowledge and celebrate the people in your life, talk to them, honestly speak what's in your heart and mind. You never know if today you will breathe your last breath.

139. No excuses

We are not all created equal and life is not fair. What are equal are the excuses for failure everyone else has and the one you made up in your head!

140. Fear

We must acknowledge and accept that the world's entire population, civilized as well as primitive, lives primarily in a state of having to confront some kind of fear. We spend our lives on a quest for finding or creating one form of security or another against things we perceive as threats of all kinds. We need to understand and learn how to deal with its inevitable presence and not be overwhelmed by something that is nothing more than a preempted thought about an unknown reality.

141. Your Creative Imagination

I visited Ripley's Believe It or Not Museum in Saint Petersburg, Florida, when my youngest son, Logan, was nine years old. He was an honor student, and I was proud of the extraordinary things he had already accomplished. On our visit to the museum, what impressed him the most was a sculpture located at the entrance. It was the first piece that we saw as we entered. It was a most unusual work of art. It represented a life-sized sculpture of a man pulling his mule in the most basic of endeavors: work. Both the man and the mule were formed from pieces of junk, things that people normally discard. They included balls, bent spoons, tin cans, sections of broken dolls, pieces of plastic, a cue stick, a section of a broomstick, candles, a broken bat, and every imaginable piece of trash that you could find. You name it, and you probably would have found it in the sculpture.

Every piece represented life experiences working and fitting together perfectly, all joining in unison to create eyes, lips, muscles, nose, ears, and all parts of the body. Both the man and the mule were beautiful interpretations of human and animal anatomies. What an amazing thought process and creativity the artist must have had to conceive such a masterpiece. I can imagine the critical and degrading thoughts and comments he had to endure from others who just did not understand, as he went around collecting the refuse components that ultimately became this beautiful work of art. It obviously didn't matter to him what others thought. He was too busy with his vision of what he wanted to create, even if it was done with nothing more than other people's trash.

It doesn't matter what building blocks you started with. What counts is what you are able to do with them. The real prize, or what some would call the gold medal or championship title, is hidden and part of the pleasure of achievement within your imagination.

142. Just Go For It

Sometimes, the only way to go is to set what may seem like unrealistic goals and just go for them, buoyed by ignorance and enthusiasm! Sometimes you can do all sorts of things when you don't know you can't do them!

143. Why?

The response to this word of "because," limits you, and keeps you from understanding the many variables involved in the occurrence of any circumstance. As a child, you said and heard it often. As an adult, it comes back to haunt you. You can sabotage the potential to discover and create new possibilities because of this word. Don't let doubt, negative words or thoughts keep you from living, enjoying and acquiring the things you can do or want in your life.

144. Balance

Everything in the universe is affected by proper balance. Nature, finance, athletes, music, art, including life itself and every other intellectual or physical skill. Your knowledge, above all, may be the most important thing affected by this, because you can never acquire as much knowledge as you will undoubtedly lack.

145. Stay on Course

We are creatures of habit. Once on any given path, we tend to follow it with consistency. When one thought arises, another thought follows. If the first thought springs from a positive seed, subsequent thoughts hold true. Do not become disillusioned by subjectivity. Hold on tight and do not allow even one doubt keep you from staying on course.

146. Do It with a Smile

When you hate or resent facing up to something that you need or have to do, you are creating an opponent within yourself that can destroy not only your will to see it through, but also the final outcome.

147. Day By Day

How can I know if I'm making the right decisions and on the right path? Every day that has passed holds the answer! To want to know is a delusion, to not know is useless.

To see the truth beyond doubt, I must flow and move with the freedom of the wind. Its movement is neither good nor not good.

148. Things Not Going Your Way?

It's interesting to note that you can't start your car if the battery cable is connected to only the positive. You must also connect the negative cable. Life, too, is connected to both sides. We must learn to take the good along with the bad. The master understands the death of a caterpillar is the birth of a butterfly. Be the master in your life.

A most important maxim is "There is no disaster that can't become a blessing, and no blessing that can't become a disaster." People refer to karma as destiny, but in fact, the word actually translates as "action and reaction."

As you accept these facts, you can appreciate that any situation—physical, mental, or emotional—is subject to the yin and yang. The more you understand and are in harmony with your own mind and body, the more you can be in balance with all things. This is not necessarily to control, but to understand better how to adapt to the adversity, appreciate and accept the circumstance. This harmony is the first step to staying in control by going with the flow.

This balance we all need relates to your life in every way. From the need to balance your budget to balancing your emotions, always consider both sides of every decision and occurrences.

149. Zen

The word "Buddha" means "awareness" or "enlightened". Zen is a Japanese form of Buddhism that emphasizes meditation. Zen aims, through meditation, to realize the emancipation of one's mind. It offers a method of self-searching, self-awareness, and self-control. Slow down. Take the time to invest in your greatest asset. Yourself!

150. Remove It

We all have something in our lives, just like a small pebble in our shoe that is constantly bothering us and that keeps us from moving forward efficiently. If we ignore, it will hinder us or create blister that can effectively stop us in our tracks.

It could be something, someone, or even your own thoughts, that are slowing you down. STOP! Find it, remove it, or it will keep you from the distraction-free state of mind you seek and from arriving at where you need to be, to reach your goals.

151. Acceptance

By realizing and accepting that what *is* can't be undone because it already *is*, we can accept what *is* and also accept what is *not*. That is also the moment we will understand fully what we could have done, as well as know what we need to do, and to appreciate that sometimes, regardless of what we do, certain things will always be as they *are*.

152. Discover the Self

Being is more important than busyness; self-discovery is the most worthy of respect. Achieving this is the way to open ones consciousness, open your awareness.

153. Empower Yourself

In today's world filled with so much hatred, violence and abuse of all kinds, the need to understand, be trained and efficient in a practical mental, physical and emotional reality defense system, is a priceless commodity that you can't afford not to possess and have at your disposal.

154. Life's Balance

The Yin and Yang of life dictates there will be birth and death, growth and deterioration, creation and destruction, war and peace. This is a part of all things, our physical bodies, plants, trees, flowers and everything in nature. It is an inescapable cycle of gain and loss, and is part of the life of every individual.

155. Don't You Stop

Why do so few reach the goals they set for themselves? I discovered early in life that most people lack a sincere commitment and the willingness to fight at all cost for the things they say they will do, want or hope for in life. When faced with difficulties or things don't go exactly as they planned or desired, they give up on their initial objectives or dreams.

Nothing in life is perfect or will come to pass without challenges, obstacles or some sort of pain. The more meaningful, valuable and worthwhile is the journey you set in front of you or have chosen, the more you will have to fight to make it come to fruition. Your path, be it in the form of a business, job, career, family, love, or any other objective, will be a rollercoaster ride. Don't let the adversity you will face, that is an integral part of all things, make you falter on your course.

When you truly feel the energy in your heart and mind, don't let impatience, anxiousness and confusion created by your thoughts keep you from following the road you chose. Keep feeding the flame that is the catalyst that forges your inspirations, destiny and purpose. Live fully, and enjoy the interaction with people and the opportunities you have been given on this earth.

156. Learn To Use the Power of Fear!

At times, when you have been through a frightening moment or emergency such as a traffic mishap or a close call, your natural survival instincts cause you to react instinctively. You may have felt "butterflies" in your gut, or an adrenalin rush. You could have even found yourself trembling after the event or danger has passed. You can have this same kind of a reaction before an event as well as after.

I realized long ago that the "butterflies" we feel in our guts is not fear. It is the body's reaction to a stressful situation as it pumps adrenaline, dopamine and endorphins to better cope with the moment. This feeling of nervousness and its reaction, especially at high levels, can be beneficial. The secret is to practice and acquire the ability to channel it or let it flow to increase your strengths and not hinder them.

When the mind realizes there is eminent danger, it will begin to release chemicals into your system that can be associated with fear. But when the event takes us by surprise, our mind is too busy with incoming information causing these chemicals to be automatically used more efficiently. In both cases, the ability to control and to focus correctly the benefits they create is of utmost importance. Just as an uncontrolled supersized water hose can knock down the user and spray its precious fluid erratically and uselessly, a controlled stream will do the perfect job of putting out the fire. In the case of firefighters, their drills and practice of maintaining control gives them the ability to do the job efficiently.

You can practice your control in using this adrenaline and its energy with something as simple as running. Set a tough but reasonable goal with an intense activity. Don't let exhaustion or fatigue let you give up.

As you improve, set goals to push yourself to higher levels. Talk and think yourself through that period where your body starts to tell you it wants to stop. Start to feel the rush and channel it to pick up the pace. Practice controlling your physical balance and innate fear of heights by using balance beams at different levels. Be creative in ways to work with and apply this to whatever your own goal is.

Behaviorists may call the initial reaction to possible injury one of "fight or flee". This is an instinctive reaction that we all have. We need to recognize it and be prepared to act. Police, airline pilots, military, all train to recognize the instinctive "fight or flee" reaction and to overcome fear with logic.

157. Pass It On

When you receive a helping hand or a favor from a stranger or anyone, be thankful to the Universal Force. Show your gratitude and keep the positive energy alive and flowing by passing it forward times two and doubling the good turn. We are all interconnected by both good and bad energy. Do your best to multiply your positive vibrations as they pass through you.

The simple meaning of the word mitzvah is command. It appears in various forms with that meaning about 300 times in the Five Books of Moses. People do "Pay it forward" for total strangers who pay for the next person in line, or who do other good deeds. Perhaps it is a command, but one that many people do because they think it is right for them to do.

158. Who's Responsible

We must take responsibility for our actions and our circumstances.

We must take steps to improve ourselves daily. You have the ability and power to create a better "you". Do it for yourself, for those you love, and just to make a better world. Find the courage in yourself to do it. You CAN do it.

Remember that the failure in the attempt to reach any goal is caused by lack of willpower, lack of purpose and courage, lack of a sense of commitment and responsibility, giving up at the first sign of hardship, and lacking self-confidence, or enthusiasm.

Don't expect a lot from others, and be willing to give of yourself. Stand up, take responsibility. Your life depends on you.

159. A Wall or A Road

Do not fall victim to what failure looks like on the surface. Your failures will appear to be like obstacles. Big stones on the road you must travel, stones that can create a wall if you stop to dwell on them. If you stare and look at them long enough, they will, by themselves, create a barrier to your purpose, one that will stop and destroy your self-confidence. One that will bring to a halt the enthusiasm you carry with you. Instead, see them as the material you need to put together your goals.

You must use these stones as a foundation to strengthen the ground that you must walk on and where you build your successes. Use your self-confidence as fuel to swing the hammer of purpose to smash them down. Step on them with the shoes of commitment. Level them with the vision of what you have planned. Never stop or give up. Keep working tirelessly, without concern as to how big they appear. Their size will, in turn, determine how large and solid and firm the road that will take you to your dreams will be.

160. Live For Today

As we think about some of the things that occurred on a particular day in our past, we failed to appreciate, as it was happening, how in what seems like the blink of an eye it would one day be 10, 15 or 20 years ago. Enjoy every second of the moment.

161. The Tree of Life

Remember to water the tree between your ears. It is connected to your real roots. They are the foundation to the quality and strength of the branches that make up who you are, who you will become and the fruit that you will bear.

162. Relax, Take That Break

As you work hard and strive for improvement or perfection in your chosen sport, activity or life, remember the law of yin and yang. There is a time to work and a time to rest. That certain something that differentiates you and makes you have that drive to succeed, can also be your downfall. Practice balance in all you do! Take advantage of the fact your body may be tired, strained or injured. Use this time to meditate and concentrate your energies to help your body's natural healing capabilities.

Take that moment to reorganize and sharpen your tools, review or lay out plans and goals with all aspects of your life. Repeat them in your mind and practice the activity, movement or drill in your thoughts first. Program the computer and equipment that is your mental and physical being so you can better use all your natural capabilities to attain your goal!! Your thoughts are your control panel to experience this life you live, learn and practice how to use it.

163. Destructive Trio

Compulsion, depression and addiction seem to go together and work off of each other. Once one jumps in, the others have a tendency to follow. They all manifest in the combination of thoughts and emotions. This is why practicing self-control of the least kind can build up to help you with these more crucial and destructive conditions.

164. We Are Constantly Evolving

Whenever I'm counseling teenagers and young adults about making drastic decisions about anything that will affect their life, I remind them of the fact that when they were 10 they thought very differently than when they were teenagers, and as they're in their twenties they will also think differently and their views will continue to change as they grow older and older.

Your likes, dislikes, your views and choices about any given circumstance will change dramatically from childhood to young adult to mature adult.

The knowledge and experiences you have and accumulate along the way should give you a different perspective about every single subject you encounter.

If this is not so, you have wasted the years you have lived.

We must allow and appreciate the lessons and the changes that the universe and our lives will inevitably have on us. Whether they are constructive or destructive will depend on us.

165. A Revelation

The invisible mystery that we call Universal Intelligence, Divine Intelligence, or God is revealed and teaches you about its Force and presence in the experiences and circumstances of your life. You must be observant and pay close attention.

166. Focus on the Positive

The ability to focus can be a tremendous asset, but it can also keep us from not noticing what's really important. There is a video called "Invisible Gorilla", where you are asked to watch a basketball game and see how many times the ball exchanges hands. During the event a man in a hairy gorilla costume walks across the court and beats his chest.

Amazingly enough, when asked if they saw anything odd, the majority of people fail to see the gorilla because their attention was focused elsewhere. In life some of us are so busy complaining on how life sucks and focusing on whatever bad is happening that we fail the see the good things that we could use in our favor and are really important and beneficial to us.

167. Change Yourself

When wanting someone to improve their life the way you feel would benefit them, be sure that your intentions are not really to benefit you. Let them be who they choose to be. Either they change or they don't change, but you can change by acquiring the ability to accept and be at peace with who they choose to be, even if it means having to break ties with them!

168. Live and Learn

Knowledge is acquired by memorization and recall of circumstances and events. Wisdom is achieved through struggle, hardships and unpleasant experiences.

169. Compassionate Lies

How many times do you not answer someone's question truthfully and honestly because you don't want to hurt their feelings, insult or anger them? How often do you make yourself miserable because you don't speak up in situations that you need to confront but are "afraid" to face?

Your reasoning of being kind, caring or compassionate to others, or just fear, makes you not only insincere as you lie your way out of saying what's truthfully in your heart or just to avoid confrontation. Now others see you as someone you are not since they see and judge you by what you tell them you think and by what you say and do! You are giving them misinformation, their view of you and of your character is based on a lie

How many times are people going to offer, promise or state that they are going to do something and then don't show, or come up with the stupidest excuses of why they didn't follow through? The worst is when they hear you could use a favor and offer themselves and won't take no for an answer. The feeling of generosity and benevolence and immediate gratification they feel and are trying to make you feel is not only worthless, but a disrespectful action to what they really feel about you as well as well as their own character.

When you speak honestly and from your heart, you give people the gift of the beauty of relating to the real you. A friendship, relation or conversation of any kind cannot become a reality, thrive or last long if it is based on lies or do not represent the real you and the truths you are committed to!! Your concern of how anyone will misinterpret what you say is irrelevant. Besides, every time you speak to ten people they each in some way take what you said with ten different interpretations based on their own emotions and fears.

If you don't like something someone said, or they ask you "your honest opinion" don't tell them what you think they want to hear, speak what your mind and heart feel. Do yourself and others a favor and base your relations on truth!

A friend may tell you things you want to hear. A close friend will tell you what you need to hear. A best friend will tell you the truth always, and completely.

170. Be Generous

Possessiveness makes us cling tightly to what we have. But what you give comes back to you. It is an investment that pays high dividends. Be generous with your time, friendship, hugs, compliments, love, and praise.

Happiness and wealth don't always go together, but happiness and a generous spirit are almost inseparable! Amazing joy, freedom, and fulfillment come when we choose to live with a generous spirit.

The Golden Rule was known to ancients globally. The Bible, Matthew 7:12 mentions this: *Do to others whatever you would like them to do to you. This is the essence of all that is taught in the law and the prophets.* The same was known in the Talmud, by Confucius and Buddhism.

171. Turn Your Brain On

We experience and enjoy our lives in two ways, our physical and mental performance and our capabilities. We have at one time or another witnessed or even experienced how an individual with a physically strong robust and healthy body can, through neglect, abuse, drugs, alcohol, diet or indifference, transform his body into a pathetically weak, frail, useless shell of its former self.

We have also seen examples of this in reverse as someone improves themselves to become a champion or to have success in whatever they choose, commit and passionately work toward, through what they eat, drink, practice, and how they care for their bodies. Our mental or intellectual abilities are also molded, shaped and created through the same process. The brain, the mind, the thoughts it creates, all drive and direct the body. Our attitude, feelings, emotions and abilities will be transformed by the quality of the thoughts we create, nurture, hold true to and practice.

Prepare and follow a training regimen and diet that will bring out the best in you. Begin by consuming this healthy mental snack. Enjoy it and use it as fuel to start you on your individual quest.

172. R.I.P.

We are exposed to death all around us, albeit the majority of the time from a distance, in movies or on the news.

Sometimes it comes closer to home, in the passing of a relative or acquaintance, usually someone older. We accept it's real, but we try our best to ignore its reality, its presence in our lives.

The Grim Reaper makes himself known and reminds us of his power over us when someone close to us is on his list and he comes for them. We do our best to try and avoid looking him in the eye, as if maybe he'll forget about us or let us skip our turn. We try to think that we're immune. But we know that one day, it will be our turn.

You stare at him every day, when you look into the mirror. He's standing right behind you, looking right back at you, because any day can be your turn. Unless we're lucky, we don't die suddenly, instead we are slowly dying minute by minute.

As we look through old pictures of ourselves, we see our childhood and a time long past. As we reach adulthood, we see ourselves begin to deteriorate, day by day, as we see our countenance aging, our demeanor slowly looking more decrepit and worn as time passes.

That Grim Reaper has time, he waits, yet at the same time, he is slowly taking us, bit by bit, breath by breath. Every so often, he tries to do something to help speed things up. He has others to visit! You're not the only one who's on his list.

Don't let him scare you, look him right in the eye, grab him by his cheeks, pull him close, give him a big kiss and tell him, "Go sit down, I'm always ready, but I'll call you when I need you".

173. Until The Last Bell Rings

Everyone enters the competition ring, competition of any kind or of life itself, with the desire to overcome the challenge, to achieve, to win. But once the bell rings, most seem to start coasting, we leave it up to the judges, fate or chance and wait for the final decision to see if we won or succeeded.

True champions, real winners, don't wait; they attack with everything they have at their disposal. They commit totally, focus on their intent and consistently go for it with every fiber of their being. They don't hesitate nor let doubt and fear of negative consequences slow them down or stop them in their tracks.

Whatever you decide to take on or want in life, be willing to give it all you've got from start to finish and then some, or die trying. Never let fate or chance decide your future.

174. The Power of Potential

The energies you possess can be compared to the power of electricity. When we didn't realize its existence, it lay dormant for hundreds of years but, as we learned about its energy, potential and how to use it, we have improved our lives in countless ways. Electricity still has the capability to hurt or even kill us, but when used wisely, it is an indispensable ally.

The ability to accept that you are bound by certain laws of nature and truths is an important part of living a satisfactory existence. To believe that some greater power or force is in control and we are subject to it seems hard to accept. Ultimately, we strive to control ourselves as well as the things around us.

My father believed that God is always in control. At the time, this seemed to me that he was giving in to whatever the circumstances dictated. But then I witnessed how calmly he dealt with problems, how his strong conviction and what he believed in gave him the ability to overcome many obstacles. You can't control everything, and yet, you can control your thoughts about how you will deal with things. If an idea or a belief can help you have peace of mind and deal with what is happening around you, then you should certainly appreciate it as a benefit.

Use the power of your beliefs in your potential to help you overcome whatever you confront. Don't let doubt or fear keep you from experiencing the joy of success. To believe in the possibility of having a dream come true is what makes life interesting.

175. Remain Calm, Stay In Control

When you experience or fall into a bad situation or problem, react just like you would do if you fell into deep, dangerous waters, don't focus on how deep it is, relax, remain calm and move systematically. Don't let yourself be drowned by fear. Focus on swimming to the top, flow with the current of the Force you are in, keep your cool.

Tap into the courage that is part of your makeup and is as powerful as any fear you may confront. Respond with the confidence that you can and will survive. The more you face and manage fear, the more courage you will create to deal when life challenges you.

176. A Pat on the Back

Nothing motivates, encourages and inspires someone to do better, work harder at any task, or succeed than a simple compliment or recognition for their efforts.

177. The Balance of Good and Bad

The more experiences you have in life, the more you will see that nothing is just good or bad. It is both. The love you have for your children, your significant other, your pets or material things, will bring you as much happiness as it will pain.

You will worry, hurt and suffer as much as you will enjoy, rejoice and be happy for everything and everyone you experience in your life. When you can accept this yin and yang law of balance in all things, you will appreciate every moment and every emotion that it contains and you will see the beauty of life and find contentment.

178. Have No Regrets

1. re-gret: A feeling of disappointment or distress about something that one wishes could be different. To remember with a feeling of longing, loss, sorrow or mourn.

We often wish we could have changed a decision we made or eliminate a particular event from our lives, but win or lose, when something comes to pass, we must find a way to accept it so we can move forward. Appreciate a yin yang approach that everything in life can be as detrimental as it is beneficial to you. This will enable you to take advantages of the possibilities that can be found in what may seem at first like a disaster.

Our lives have happy, as well as painful, frightening and traumatic moments. No one is exempt from this! If you can see that everything serves its purpose, you won't get trapped in the thought that if things had been different they would be better.

Things are what they are! You are what must flow, blend and be pliable. This is the way to be in harmony with events, people and things without the thought of a "good or bad" label to confuse you.

We acquire some strength as well as lose some as we grow, gain experience and get older. Both our minds and bodies are continuously changing. My life, and I am sure yours, both are full of moments that no sane person would pick as something they would willingly choose or like to experience. But I wouldn't change a thing! I have no regrets!!

My experiences taught me the lessons and gave me the strength that have carried me through life and have given me an understanding of who I am today. It gives me a sense of accomplishment and pride that distinguishes who I am.

Take the time to review your life from this point of view, and I'm sure you will find a half smile/snicker appearing on your lips of all the things you have been through and survived. This will be the catalyst for you to "suck it up" and continue your quest for your gold!

179. Five Steps to True Learning

You may feel frustrated at times about your progress. Don't beat yourself up! You and everyone else on Earth must take the same path. You can regulate slightly how soon you reach particular goals, but we must all follow the same road map and pass the same locations!

You may well have hurdles in your way. You may learn something, but not understand it. You may learn something and understand it, but not be able to do it. You could do all these things, but not be able to do what you learned while under pressure. You could be successful even under pressures, but still fail to apply what you learned and can do to your own life. That is the final step, to do and to apply it to your own life.

Whatever goals you have, you will have these experiences as well. To complete all the steps, of learning, understanding, accomplishing, doing it under pressures and also applying what you learned in your own life, as an individual, this is growing and moving to the next level, to experience "Zen" or "Being in the Zone".

180. Commit

You must be willing to commit and sacrifice all that you are and have today, for who you can be and want to achieve tomorrow!

181. It's Not Over

*E*very time you encounter disappointment or experience a loss, remember the vibrations of life are constantly moving to a negative and positive flow. Realize that your story isn't over. Things will change you will rise to a situation better then what you lost.

Never give up. Continue on a forward course, and expect good things to be right around the corner. If your focus is on what you don't have, it will keep you stagnant in the same place. But when you seek for and expect to find something good, you will be able to recognize the opportunity when it comes your way.

182. Expect the Best

There will be moments of successes as well as failures in your life. What you imagine, believe, and expect, influences your ability to blend with the ups and downs and take advantage of whatever opportunities you are presented with. Having the vision of what you want and the courage to go for it when the opportunity arises, is crucial to achieving your goals.

183. You Help Create

We create the circumstances for successes, as well as for failures, by what we think and what we focus on. What you say and believe and what you imagine, influences your ability to blend with and take advantage of whatever opportunities you are presented with. Having the courage to take chances and not fear failure, is crucial to achieving your goals.

184. Bit by Bit

Every great achievement and success you reach in your life is comprised, and will come about, in small daily increments of victories as well as failures.

185. Who Knows?

Until our last day on Earth, there will always be things we haven't learned or can do, and there will always be someone that knows and can teach us something we may not know. We have a tendency to compartmentalize people and consider their worth by just one particular appearance or judgment by which we categorize them. We may think, well I'm the parent, or I'm the teacher, or I'm their boss, or I have a degree.

The fact is, that someone can be younger than you, have less money, less education, a lower position at work, less experience in a particular field of expertise, be of a different race ethnic group or gender, and still know or have information that you are not privy to that may save your life or take you to a higher level with a particular task or challenge.

Keep an open mind and realize that we all have different gifts, talents, knowledge and experience that make up the total of who we are. Sometimes the student learns from the teacher, sometimes the teacher learns from the student and sometimes, the least likely source can be filled with a treasure of valuable information.

186. A Subconscious Power

Hypnosis has shown us how the power of suggestion into our subconscious minds and thought process can be programmed to alter our conscious mind and what we believe is possible.

We have heard how ordinary individuals, under a form of self-hypnosis triggered by an emotional desire and their thoughts, have performed superhuman heroic feats.

By releasing hormones and endorphins, this can multiply the body's strengths and abilities tenfold. They were somehow empowered to complete an action or accomplish what would normally be considered a humanly impossible feat in saving someone or themselves during catastrophic events.

Don't cut yourself short. Your being, physically as well as mentally, is an amazing creation.

187. A Conundrum

Which is greater, the hatred you have for the situation you are experiencing now, or the fear of standing up and starting on the road that will take you on an unknown journey to something new?

188. Pass It Forward

When you receive a helping hand or a favor from a stranger or anyone, be thankful to the Universal Force. Show your gratitude and keep the positive energy alive and flowing by passing it forward times two and doubling the good turn. We are all interconnected by both good and bad energy. Do your best to multiply yours as it passes through you.

189. Mastering the Self

Training in the Martial Arts is not particularly practiced for the purpose of defending yourself or fighting in the street. Realistically, the greater majority of us will rarely if ever have physical encounters of any type, and will actually seldom if ever use it in that type of situation.

We do, however, often have daily battles with our thoughts, the decisions we have to make, as well as with verbal and situational encounters with life and with others.

The same sense of mental, emotional, and sometimes physical control that would be necessary in one is equally as necessary in the other. The mind and body will need to calmly and efficiently react to and handle stressful situations.

It's not about learning forms, katas or any particular technique, but instead it's about practicing your ability to be able to coordinate your mind and body to remain composed and perform efficiently when someone is trying to overpower you and potentially hurt or injure you while aggressively attacking you in a non-choreographed and as realistic as possible situation.

190. Appreciate This Day

As we think about some of the things that occurred on a particular day in our past, we failed to appreciate as it was happening, how, in what seems like the blink of an eye, it would one day be 10, 15 or 20 years ago. Enjoy every second of the moment.

191. Follow Your Passion

Envision, love, commit, and have passion for what you seek. Never waiver from your goals, or let your resolve grow weary and you will reach success.

192. Relax, You Can Use The Break

As you work hard and strive for improvement or perfection in your chosen sport, activity or life, remember the law of yin and yang. There is a time to work and a time to rest. That certain something that differentiates you and makes you have that drive to succeed can also be your downfall. Practice balance in all you do! Take advantage of the fact your body may be tired, strained or injured. Use this time to meditate and concentrate your energies to help your body's natural healing capabilities.

Take a moment to review or lay out plans and goals with all aspects of your life. Repeat them in your mind and practice the activity, movement or drill in your thoughts first. Program the computer and equipment that is your mental and physical being so you can better use all your natural capabilities to attain your goal!! Your thoughts are your control panel to experience this life you live, learn and practice how to use it.

193. The Art of Love

In music, poetry, art, and all the greatest creations in the world, Love for another has been the greatest catalyst! Without someone, your children, spouse, family, soul mate or even a pet, there is created a void that we usually try to fill with alcohol, drugs, or even food. Daily we hear of wealthy, famous, and seemingly successful people destroying their lives or themselves because they have ignored or neglected this aspect of their existence. Love yourself first, and then share that with someone. Life is meaningless without passion. Don't let yourself neglect or take for granted this most important part of your life.

194. We Should Be Evolving

Whenever I'm counseling teenagers and young adults about making drastic decisions about anything that will affect their life, I remind them of the fact that when they were 10, they thought very differently than when they were teenagers and as they're in their twenties, they will also think differently and their views will continue to change as they grow older and older.

Your likes, dislikes, your views and choices about any given circumstance should change dramatically from childhood to young adult to mature adult.

The knowledge and experiences you have and accumulate along the way should give you a different perspective about every single subject you encounter.

If this is not so you have wasted the years you have lived.

We must allow and appreciate the lessons and the changes that the universe and our lives will inevitably have on us. Whether they are constructive or destructive will depend on us.

195. Winning or Losing

Your confusion about the answer starts with the misconception that you are in competition with others. You're not! The yin yang of life dictates that you will always be a loser because there will always be someone who on any given day will beat you. You will always be a winner because from day one of whatever your endeavor there will be someone you can crush.

YOU, are your number one adversary and the person who you must challenge and defeat on a daily basis. You can use others to gauge your progress or lack thereof but that's it.

Remember, it's not just training and strengthening your physical abilities; it's strengthening and developing your character that counts.

The people that let their ego control who they are trying to become will never reach their most valuable goal, self-improvement.

Others will ultimately see you for how hard you tried and how far you progressed, not what you did or didn't accomplish. The fact you failed the first few times should serve as a drum roll of tense anticipation to the climax of your achievement.

196. A Revelation

The invisible mystery that is The Universal Intelligence, Wisdom, Divine Intelligence, or God is revealed and teaches you about its Force and presence in the experiences and circumstances of your life. You must be observant and pay close attention.

197. Focus on the Positive

The ability to focus can be a tremendous asset, but it can also keep us from not noticing what's really important. There is a video called "Invisible Gorilla", where you are asked to watch a basketball game and see how many times the ball exchanges hands. During the event, a man in a hairy gorilla costume walks across the court and beats his chest.

Amazingly enough, when asked if they saw anything odd, the majority of people fail to see the gorilla. In life some of us are so busy complaining on how life sucks and focusing on whatever bad is happening that we fail the see the good things that we could use in our favor and are really important and beneficial to us.

198. Reviewing Your Day

This is the perfect Ying and yang to use every daily. Whenever you feel like saying, "this has been a terrible day for me," go back and review it again. Think about the other things that are more valuable and really count, like breathing, seeing, walking, and just being alive.

Go back and say, "Some things were bad, but some things were good." Now you will see that your glass is half full and you have tomorrow to finish filling it to the top.

199. Thinking Positive

Most of us are familiar with or have heard about the book *The Power of Positive Thinking* by Norman Vincent Peale. It has become a popular self-help guide that he published in 1952. He emphasized that people should trust that a Universal Force and God's higher power is always with them.

He realized that when we affirm, visualize, and believe that this power is working on and can affect our lives, we energize that belief, actualize that force and connection, and can achieve astonishing results.

200. The Special You

We all have a different quality, talents and gifts which we can use in life. We are all in different situations and circumstances but we all possess the same potential and capabilities to improve and rise to higher levels. Don't compare yourself to others. Carefully seek out and discover what you have at your disposal that you can use to help yourself as well as others to conquer your personal goals and achieve your true purpose. Sink all of your commitment into that. We must take responsibility for doing the best we can with what we have individually been given in our lives.

201. You Will Survive

Our problems, the negative unwanted, inevitable circumstances, or the depression that may accompany it, is like a powerful current in a flooded river. We don't voluntarily jump in; we somehow fall, or get pushed in. But once we're in our choice of what we need to do becomes clear! We need to get out of what can pull us down and drown us.

Some of us will take immediate action, do everything within our power to save ourselves and reach firm ground again. Some are able to make it on their own; others may need a helping hand. As you see others that have succeeded it inspires you to try harder, not give up, or let fear create the catatonic state that can freeze you and make you another statistic.

You are not the only one that has or will fall in to this river. Don't let yourself be overwhelmed, reach deep inside and draw on the courage you need to accomplish the goal that is before you. Do whatever it takes. You can and will survive! Never give in and never give up! It is only life testing you. Your experience will make you stronger!

202. Free Your Mind

Every day, we see discoveries, advancements, and achievements in every field of endeavor that we previously felt certain were not possible. We have no idea how far we can go, nor the potential we each possess to reach new dimensions.

Therefore, let's give our thoughts, ideas, and creativity complete freedom to take us in whatever direction they can imagine.

203. You Get It?

You can't expect to receive all you can get if you're not willing to give it all you got!

204. Learn and Teach

In life, true to the Yin Yang principal, you will help, teach, mentor or be an example to someone else. But from the day we are born, we depended upon someone to help us and guide us. At the beginning, it may have been your parents, later it could have been a teacher, family member or mentor. There will always be a need for someone we can look up to and learn from. Sometimes this guidance may not be given to you in positive way; we can learn not only from our own mistakes but also by observing other people's mistakes. You can't make every mistake yourself. This would be detrimental to your life, so you should be observant of others, not only what they do well, but also when they do things that cause them harm.

205. Flow

Unpleasant moments will definitely be a part of life. We need to be resilient. Webster defines "resiliency" as, the ability to recover quickly from an illness, change, or misfortune; buoyancy. Go with the flow and be in harmony with yourself and the circumstances that confront you.

206. A Universal Intelligence

Everything you want or need to know, and the knowledge of how to create or achieve, it is within your grasp. You are part of the Universal, Divine Intelligence and Wisdom that is one with and creates all things. You must shut off the chatter that occupies your mind and thoughts to tap into and listen to what it can reveal to you. Slow down, let your mind be silent, in this introspecting peace and through meditation you will discover and learn more than you could ever imagine.

207. Adapt

You have an ingrained human characteristic of the ability to adapt to whatever the situation. This gives you tremendous powers and abilities. To tap into them, you must trust and believe this! Your fears, doubts and lack of faith squash your potential and keep you from being your best now and in the future.

208. Riding the Wave

You can't ride the wave if you fear falling in the water.

209. Discover the Real You

With whatever emotion involved, be it fear, doubt, hatred, compassion, love or any other, we all have a Breaking Point. We never know what our ability to tolerate or handle a situation or limit is until we are put in the position or circumstances that will give us the opportunity to discover it.

Don't cower or back away from the chance to open up, learn, look inside yourself and risk your ego, self-esteem or a false self-identity. This is the only way to grow and find out who you really are or what your true capabilities could be when it really counts.

210. Facing Fear Creates Courage

Every day, you deal with two important factors: your physical and mental state and well-being. Life is a constant battle, mentally, emotionally, and verbally, we struggle with our own bodies, illnesses, thoughts, doubts, fears, decisions, family, friends, acquaintances, fellow workers, and even strangers.

Throughout our lives, we are faced with physical and emotional situations that can be both frightening and painful. They can manifest themselves in different ways and at any time. You begin your attempt to avoid or protect yourself early in life against these threatening occurrences. You don't like the feelings of fear caused by them.

Fear can present itself and influence us in different ways. Real fear is the fear of real injury, pain illness or the real possibility of eminent death. Nervous fear is the fear of the unknown, failure, or public humiliation; like walking in front of a large audience to speak, perform or compete. Both physical fear and nervous fear are very real and require real courage to face. We all have fear as a natural emotion to help us survive. Don't let your fears keep you from living life to the fullest

Life is filled with uncertainty and stress, but life also holds fantastic opportunities and possibilities. We all face different kinds of battles in our lives. When you confront these real-life situations, you must focus on developing self-confidence, both mental and emotional and learn to remain flexible. Use your inner strength and self-control to help you conquer your fear, control stress in all aspects of life, flow with life's situation, and recognize and seize opportunities.

211. The River That is Life

The journey to reach your goal or purpose in life involves flowing steadily down a river that you must travel in order to arrive at your destination. At times, it will be pleasant and serene, but you will inevitably encounter some strong currents and rough waters. It can be an exciting adventure and an enjoyable ride if you let its flow take you with its force to all the strange new circumstances, places and people you will meet.

The more you struggle to control or fight the current, the harder your journey will become and the longer it will take you to reach your destination. When you feel the pull of an inconvenience or difficult situation, you must flow with it and be in the now.

Be one with what you are doing and where you are at the moment. The lessons you learn and what you are experiencing is part of the trip and will help you appreciate and enjoy the destination that much more. Never lose the vision of what you are trying to achieve, but remember that the journey is an integral and the most important part of reaching any goal. The ability to be in harmony with every aspect of life is empowering, refreshing and releasing.

212. Life's Gauge

Your life is not measured by your talents, exceptional abilities, or lack thereof. It is measured and dependent on your strength and willingness to persevere. By realizing and accepting your own mortality, and how short and valuable your existence here is, you will be able to appreciate, release and use the empowering force that lies trap behind your fear of failure, loss, and death.

213. A Guiding Light

No matter how brightly our light shines to help others find their way, we will always be in need of the light that helps us out of our own darkness.

214. Just Go For It

The more times you swing the bat and miss, the better the chance you have of hitting a homerun. The more times you fail, the greater the chance of you succeeding. The more bad ideas that you have, the greater the chance of you coming up with a good one. It's the fear of trying and not succeeding that will be your biggest obstacle.

215. Self- Abuse or Self Control

Today's society is plagued with drugs, alcohol and crime. This is a weakness and behavior that is destroying our country. It's not any one particular drug, substance, or food that is the biggest culprit in the deterioration of the quality of our lives, it is self-abuse brought on by the lack of discipline.

We have become a generation of finger pointing, excuse oriented people. It's always someone or something else's fault. We can find dozens of reasons for whatever befalls us other than taking personal responsibility. We, each of us individually and collectively, are responsible for the life we live.

The minute you take responsibility for you, you will be empowered. It will be the moment you are no longer a slave to circumstances.

216. Imaginative Visualization

Whatever you can create in your thoughts, constantly visualize yourself as part of the picture and consistently strengthen that image emotionally with every fiber of your being, you have the potential to manifest into reality.

Julia Mancuso drew a picture of herself when she was nine years old. The picture was of Julia winning the gold medal in women's skiing. From the time she was 9 years old, she looked at that picture almost every day. In 2006 Winter Olympics at the age of 21, Julia Mancuso won the gold medal.

217. The #1 Computer

Your body and mind are the most intricate and efficient tools and computer in the world. *YOU* own it! You can use it to download, interpret, sort, retrieve and use a perpetual amount of information and knowledge. You can use it for simple everyday tasks like Facebook, e-mail and chatting with friends or you can discover yourself and create a world of new possibilities!

Every time I train, I see and feel myself in a room that monitors and controls every aspect of my movement and the purpose behind it. I control the button for stance, balance, timing, range, mobility, speed and strength and adjust them accordingly. A coach can share a program with you, but you have to push the buttons to download, interpret, sort, retrieve, and perform the task for yourself.

Every day, we see some new and remarkable innovation by people that take time, enjoy and repetitiously take advantage of and use their computers to accomplish extraordinary goals. Don't just sit on yours.

218. Commit

You must be willing to commit and sacrifice all that you are and have today for who you can be and want to achieve tomorrow.

219. Osmosis

It is better to be a fool in a land of wise men, than a wise man in a land of fools. You become like those you associate with, birds of a feather flock together.

220. Love and Passion

Webster defines "Passion" as

1: a strong feeling or enthusiasm for something or for doing something. 2: a strong emotional feeling that makes you act in a certain way 3: a strong sexual or romantic feeling for someone.

What is your passion? What inspires, drives, and motivates you, money, your job, family, friends, something else? The greatest of passions are fueled by Love! The greatest of Loves is that for another living creature. Money, accolades, fame or fortune are really meaningless without being able to share with others or with that special someone.

221. Use It or Lose It

Break your arm and put it in a cast and in 4 weeks it looks atrophied and shrunken and doesn't work till you start using it again! Any muscle tissue that does not receive stimulation and blood flow dies! Including your brain. Learn or practice a new function mentally as well as physically every day. If you don't use it, you lose it!

In music, poetry, art, and all the greatest creations in the world, Love for another has been the greatest catalyst! Without someone, your children, spouse, family, soul mate or even a pet, there is created a void that we usually try to fill with alcohol, drugs, or even food. Daily we hear of wealthy, famous, and seemingly successful people destroying their lives or themselves because they have ignored or neglected this aspect of their existence. Love yourself first, and then share that with someone. Life is meaningless without passion. Don't let yourself neglect or take for granted this most important part of your life.

222. Slow Down

Contemplation, meditation and prayer help you create a high state of awareness. By shutting off the bombardment of outside stimulus on our senses we are able to connect with a universal and divine consciousness. When you tap into this source you create the catalyst that unites your mind, your ideas, and your ability to express them.

It stimulates and brings forth the patience, knowledge and strength needed to discover the wisdom necessary to face, confront, be in harmony with, and deal with the obstacles and challenges life presents us with.

223. What Have You Done For Yourself

We create our own successes as well as failures by what we think and what we focus on. What you say and believe and what you imagine influences your ability to blend with and take advantage of whatever circumstances you are presented with. Having the courage to take chances and not fear failure is crucial to achieving your goals

You have creative abilities. The person you are, your face, hair, body, organs, every part of you was brought about by a picture or fixed image of you in a single cell. This picture slowly unfolded and grew or became objectified. Like this cell or seed, you have the ability to create ideas that can be turned into reality in any area. You just have to nurture them to maturity.

History shows us that some of the greatest discoveries and inventions were made by people that were laughed at, taunted, and ridiculed by their peers. Some of these people tried and failed dozens if not hundreds of times and yet never gave up on their dreams. Whatever goals you have or whatever challenges you may face can be conquered with your most valuable asset, your creative mind. Don't just sit back in a helpless state of mind, waiting to see what happens. When facing difficult issues or problems that we all inevitably confront, I sometimes blurt out the remark, "Well, let's see what happens." instead, "Let's make something happen." Don't let your destiny be created by fear, by apathy, or because you wouldn't at least give it your best shot. Don't let other people keep you from living out your plans to achieve.

Instead of dwelling on reasons why you can't, dwell on how you can. And there will be nothing you can't accomplish.

Commitment and hard work is the bridge between your goals and your accomplishments.

224. We Are Pure Energy

Our physical, as well as our mental being and everything on earth, is made up from positive and negative electric vibrations. Your heart can be stopped or started back up with electric shock. So can your mind. We can send this energy, either positive or negative to others at any given moment, not only through our words and actions but also through a presence.

We have all experienced up or down mood changes brought about by others or from nature itself. Dark gloomy weather or being in an enclosed dark room brings about a different feeling in us than being out on the beach in the Sun or in the garden with beautiful flowers. Grounding and connecting with the Earth and nature can boost our pain and pleasure connectors and can also stimulate our bodies to heal or create illness and disease.

This can also be brought about with our aura or the seemingly invisible energy vibrations that we constantly send out to others. We are all part of a Universal Force that we can use in both positive as well as negative ways, for good or for evil. We must consider the fact that we will attract the same energy we project.

225. Can't and Can

Don't let the things you can't do dissuade you or keep you from doing the things you can do. We all have talents and lack thereof. We all have things that we're good at and things that we're not capable of achieving. Find your niche. Discover what inspires, motivates, and drives you. Go for it with all your heart.

226. Face Life

When you experience the negative emotion of feeling insecure, scared or afraid of having to face a situation or a conversation with someone, rather than behaving like the child that hides or flees when confronted by a perceived danger, stop! Review the situation. Step forward, not back.

Figure out what you have to do. Take action. No matter how hard you try, you will never be able to hide or escape from the reality of your emotions and the things you need to do to move forward.

227. Simply Clear Your Thoughts

The solutions to the problems and challenges you encounter in life are like when someone tells you a riddle. They are both complicated, as well as simple.

You have a difficult time seeing the solution because your mind is cluttered and trying too hard. You feel that the answer, or what you need to do, has to be as complicated as the problem seems.

When you hear the answer or discover a solution, you always feel silly you didn't think of something so simple sooner.

228. Sharing Your Wisdom

The greatest lesson you can share and teach anyone is yourself. Teach by example. It is by far the best way to spread your knowledge.

229. Highest Level of Self Control

The harmony of emotions, mind and body can be experienced in different ways. In Zen, it might be described as "Being at one with the Universe." In sports, any athletic or physical endeavor, it's described by the expression "Being in the zone."

230. A Positive and Negative Flow

Negativity is part of society's evolution. Don't get caught up with the ills, pain, and suffering that exist in the world, or ask, how does God allow this. It is a necessary part of the yin and yang of life. It is, has been and always will be the other half of and responsible for man's search for a better way, life and our progress throughout history.

231. Moving Meditation

Meditation should be part of your every day. Through meditation you observe yourself. It helps you experience serenity. You need serenity to take control of your emotions.

Exercise and nutritional discipline is a system of meditation because it takes discipline to wrestle your personality into a place where it is quiet and serene. This helps you learn to center the mind.

It is one of the best ways you can connect with the universal mind intelligence and receive answers to who you are your purpose and the interdependent nature of your reality.

232. Today

As we think about some of the things that occurred on a particular day in our past, we failed to appreciate as it was happening, how in what seems like the blink of an eye, it would one day be 10, 15 or 20 years ago. Enjoy every second of the moment.

233. Your Fiercest Opponent

"I count him braver he who overcomes his desires than he who conquers his enemies; for the hardest victory is the victory over the self" Aristotle

Establish your word to yourself as law. By doing this you expand your powers. If you tell yourself or someone you will do something, whatever it may be. Do it! If you don't keep your word, your trust in yourself and your abilities in anything you do or plan are diminished or totally disappear.

Don't make promises you don't intend to keep. If you tell yourself you're going to start an exercise regiment, give up chocolates, smoking, drinking or anything else and don't follow through, you are sabotaging your character and anything else you attempt. If you have any notion that you won't follow through, don't say or promise it. Wait! Once you are fully and ready to commit, go for it and never look back. By embracing your word as law you will see your powers to manifest your life and character develop to a superior level.

234. The Force That is Life

I firmly believe we and every living thing are connected to a Universal Force, a Divine Intelligence, Energy, a God like spirit that is within and part of us and we are part of it.

Our instinctive need to identify, relate to, control and somehow possess everything in this expansive universe has created a vision in our minds of an attractive, blue eyed, long flowing hair white man to represent and be the image we relate to as God.

We fail to realize, recognize and accept that this living spirit is in every animal, insect, plant, molecule and atom that we see around us. In the air we breathe, the water that gives us life and what turns it on at birth and off at death. It is formless and yet takes on every form.

The greatest of human minds have tried their best to try to keep this life going, to create it, control it, understand it, and as hard as they work are like a newborn trying to comprehend quantum physics.

I am content to live in, be part of, enjoy, exist in and have at my disposal this force, and the use of this beautiful garden and cornucopia of bountiful things that it creates. I start my day and do my meditation every morning outside surrounded by nature; it energizes me and fills my day with positive motivating vibrations and energy.

Maybe this is the branch of the tree of knowledge that was referenced and meant to always elude and be a mystery to us.

235. Visualization

One of the keys to seeing your dreams come to pass, is to visualize achieving them in your mind's eye first.

Some of the greatest athletes of our time like gold medal skier Lindsey Vonn, volleyballs 3x gold medal duo Kerri Walsh and Misty Meyer as well as Mr Universe and film star Arnold Schwarzenegger and others said that they used visualization to see themselves executing a winning performance. This vision would permeate every fiber in their mind, body and whole being and then express and become the action.

Of course, it takes more than just visualization to see our dreams come to pass. It takes drive; it takes commitment. What I'm saying is that if you'll keep the right pictures in your imagination, seeing yourself rising higher, seeing yourself healthy and whole, is what you need to get deep down inside of you to set the course for your life. You will gain the supernatural strength and power to see those dreams and desires come to pass in your life!

236. Dying While Still Living

We seldom think about our fear of a physical death. But the death of our ego, the self we have created whom and what we think we are, haunts us every day. Our self-esteem and sense of worth need to constantly be nurtured to stay alive in us. The different challenges we take on daily make us feel alive. To not have the courage to take risk, new adventures and live life to the fullest is worse than our carnal death.

237. Beneficial Flaws

Accept and find comfort in what you may perceive as a flaw or short coming in your life. The Tao teaches that the more you have, the more you need to protect and the more you have to lose.

The higher you are, the further down you can fall. The tallest tree is the first one to get cut down. The crooked, bent tree is of no use to the woodsman so it lives a thousand years.

Be like water; don't always worry about having to make big waves. Sometimes just flow down to fill the emptiness of the smallest place. Be content and appreciate the now, who and where you are. This is the yin yang of accepting yourself and enjoying a successful existence.

238. Wisdom Road

The road to wisdom is full of turns into mystery, astonishment, and wonder.

239. Practice and Repeat

When you are practicing to perfect a skill, you perform different drills. You must be aware that repeated practice is what creates habits and there is a force created by those habits that will manifest itself in your life.

Beware to rid yourself of habits that can work against you and continue the ones that will help you move forward with a positive momentum.

240. Motivation

You're already in possession the best motivator you could have to conquer and overcome any goal, challenge or obstacle. In order to use and take advantage of it, you must focus and meditate on one thought. Your burning desire to achieve!

241. Make Your Day

You have the power to be happy, successful, and content, to enjoy every day of your life. It's as easy as creating your next thought.

242. Purpose

We do our best to make every day have purpose. It gives us a sense of accomplishment when we complete any task. Oftentimes, we get lost in the rat race of the same routine of our goals with work, family, success and perhaps a little time to relax and do what we enjoy.

Although we put it aside and often try to ignore it, we can't help but also wonder and seek an answer to the mystery of this spirit inside us that gives us life and knows our greater purpose. This can't be all there is. We're born, we breathe, we live, we love, we suffer, and we die!

Sometimes we can't help but ask ourselves, "What is our real purpose in this journey called life?" As you consume this thought and the answer that is your individual purpose, it can consume you, it devours you and you become one with it. This experience is the greatest harmony of the Yin and Yang of life. This could be where we will find answer.

243. Stay Focused On Your Intent

When trying to reach a goal, in business, competition or in your daily life, focus on intent is what will determine how far you will go or what you will achieve. If your intent is to do your best and just see what happens, that is all that will happen. To break a record, be really successful or beat a champion, you have to see beyond what lies in front of you.

Don't wait and see what others will do or have done. Set your mind, focus and especially your intent beyond what you can see or imagine. All accomplishments begin, end and are fueled with the power of your intent!

244. An Emotional Connection

What could seem like a simple smile to you, could bring someone out of a depressing and sad situation. What may seem to you like a simple compliment, could make someone feel important or special. What may seem to you like an insignificant conversation or word, could mean the world to someone that needed to hear what you might have to say. We are all different; we share different circumstances in life. We may all look different, but we all share one common denominator, and that is our emotions. Your emotions create energy and vibrations that can turn a simple encounter into a real connection or relationship.

Emotions are the substance of what other people share with us and we share with them. This is the greatest currency that we could ever possess. Connect with someone today. Either give or receive the most valuable asset you could exchange with anyone. The moment you show someone you care about them or that you need someone to care about you, you open the door to riches beyond your greatest expectations. Enrich someone's life or your own by making that powerful connection.

245. Good Vibrations

People often remark or ask me, how do I seem to come out ahead or end up winning in situations and circumstances that appeared to be stacked against me? One person said that, throughout my life even when I stepped in crap, I came up smelling like a rose.

As I have stated, every situation has the potential of being negative or positive. Wherever I find myself, my mind searches for how what is happening could be positive for me. I always try my best, to seek out and project positive vibrations even in negative circumstances.

The more you reach out, encourage, motivate, inspire, and empower others to overcome their challenges, the more those same attributes will come back to you. You will create a situation where there's always a line of people ready and willing to help you. You can harvest the same things in your life. But first, you have to start by planting the seed of giving. We are all interdependent. Start by doing something today to lift or help someone rise to a higher level. You will reap what you sow.

246. Your Word Your Credibility

In *Face Fear Create Courage*, I wrote a chapter titled "The Power of Thought" about how everything that you see around you was a thought first. The following chapter was "The Power of Words", and it states the importance of your words and how they can create positive as well as negative effects and situations in your life. To be impeccable to your word gives you credibility. The word credit derives from the word credibility. To have good credit or credibility gives you power.

It states in the Bible that God spoke a word and created everything we see. This is where the word, "Universe" comes from; it translates to "one verse". You create your world, your personal universe, with what you think and what you speak. Be true to your words, to yourself and to others and use them wisely. They are the tools that you will use to build your life, your future, your successes, as well as your failures.

247. A Clear Path

If the road or path you are on has no obstacles or challenges, it will probably not take you anywhere worthwhile or where you will grow to the person who you need to be.

248. Give It All You Got

Whatever the task, perform and hold yourself responsible to a standard much higher than anyone would ever expect from you without concern for reward for yourself, but instead for the pride of doing to the best of your ability.

249. Strength of Character

Our emotions, together with the way we respond to them, creates something we call character. It is your character that determines success or failure in your life, and character is always a work in progress. Your character is built from the words you speak and your actions. Character is the glue that holds you together and gives you strength and willingness to live by those words and back up your words and actions.

250. A Subconscious Power

Hypnosis has shown us how the power of suggestion into our subconscious minds and thought process. It can be programmed to alter our conscious mind and what we believe is possible.

We have heard how ordinary individuals, under a form of self-hypnosis triggered by an emotional desire and their thoughts, have performed superhuman heroic feats.

By releasing hormones and endorphins this can multiply the body's strengths and abilities tenfold. They were somehow empowered to complete an action or accomplish what would normally be considered a humanly impossible feat in saving someone or themselves during catastrophic events.

Don't cut yourself short. Your being, physically as well as mentally, is an amazing creation.

251. Agree to Disagree

You will never agree with anyone 100% on every issue! Not your family, friends or acquaintances. Your close friends are in the 50% range. Real friends will respect each other even when they disagree.

BERT RODRIGUEZ

252. Be Prepared

Spectacular achievements are always preceded by spectacular preparation.

253. Cooperative Strength

As much as we may feel that individuality and competition can bring out the best in someone, research has shown that an attitude of harmonious interaction, where teamwork is implemented, makes individuals grow and improve to both much higher levels and in proportion to the other members in the group. When a group has an individual trying to outdo or be better than others, his level of improvement and productivity is less.

254. Wonder and Wisdom

This is the time, the moment, the day, you can use to empower yourself to the next level.

Every piece of knowledge you acquire is part of the overall wisdom that will help your ability to achieve every circumstance and overcome the obstacles you will inevitably encounter.

Knowledge is power. From our first day on this Earth, our ability to learn helps us overcome the challenges we face.

We can learn something new each day. We could live a thousand years and not learn everything there is to know about one single subject. We will be learning until the day we die.

Always seek out this most valuable asset in life, *Knowledge*.

255. Negativity in Life

Learn to accept, appreciate, and use what at first you may perceive as negative circumstances or people who are part of your life. They are your teachers. They are here to help you learn. They help you become a stronger, better individual.

They are helping you to learn about yourself, make you strong, teaching you to create a positive from a negative. They help you to understand and accept who you are and guide you to who and where you need to be. They are giving you a gift. Be thankful for them.

256. Here Lies Your True Worth

If your word has no substance or value, neither do you!

257. The Perfect Diet

The two most important things we possess and must nourish, are our physical and mental states. Both have to be fed a nutritional diet!

258. To Have and Have Not

Appreciate both the positive and negative sides of every experience in life. They coexist and constantly complement each other. You can't have one without the other.

The hungrier you are, the more you will enjoy eating. The colder you are, the more you will see the blessing of warmth. Illness will help you appreciate good health. The more you experience, the more you will be able to share with others. The more you see how much you still have to learn, the more you will be able to teach.

259. Your Smile

There are two ways of spreading light to brighten someone's life: To be the lamp that produces it, or the mirror that reflects it.

260. Osmosis

From the day we are born, and through early childhood, we create and become the individuals we are today through the interaction, personal or otherwise, with the people we follow, admire and respect the most. This process constantly evolves as we meet and associate with more and more new people.

261. We Attract Each Other's Energy

We learn and repeat actions by relating to them and absorbing them. They then influence us by becoming part of our own mindset and habits. For this reason we need to be careful to not constantly associate ourselves with negative people or negative thoughts. They can quickly become part of our own thinking process.

Because of our natural instinct to feel empathy, we become one with the problems and negativity of others.

Motivate others, but disassociate yourself from people who are complainers, always down and never happy. Do your best to associate with the people who have a good outlook about their life, as well as with the obstacles that they may confront. Seek out those who make you laugh, pick you up, and make you feel positive, encourage and empower you.

262. Climb to the Top

If you don't make the commitment to find the courage in your heart to climb the highest mountain, you'll never get to see, enjoy and partake in all the beautiful splendor below.

263. In Its Own Time

We have all, at one time or another, felt the emotion of impatience. Be it for the cookies that smell so good to bake, for a delicious meal to be ready and served, for that physical or emotional pain and wound to heal, or for that special occasion or moment to happen.

Everything has its own chosen time to occur and complete its cycle. No amount of anxiousness, worry, or wishful desire can change the given time everything has been allotted in life. Have patience, flow and be in the moment. Everything occurs in its own due time.

264. Fear and Control

Whether it's real life circumstances, your children, your pets, or the people around you, the feeling of not having any control over them creates fear for the future, them, their safety or your own.

We seem to feel that we could, through some internal power, keep disasters or unpleasant situations from materializing. We can't! As much as we would love to control life, we are all part of a universal force that works of its own accord.

The best we can do is accept, adapt, flow and appreciate the duality of life's adversities and the wisdom of a higher Universal Intelligence that keeps everything in a harmonious order.

Trust and have faith in its wisdom and fact that every occurrence we may encounter can set us back as much as move us forward. Destroy us as much as take us to a higher level. Here is the only thing we will ever really be able to control

265. Empower Yourself

In today's world, filled with so much hatred, violence and abuse of all kinds, the need to understand, be trained and efficient in a practical mental, physical and emotional reality defense system is a priceless commodity that you can't afford not to possess and have at your disposal.

266. Equal Exchange

You acquire your greatest strengths from your worst experiences

267. We Each Define Success

When we finally overcome any obstacle or challenge we take on, we discover that what we really conquered was ourselves.

268. The Ride of Your Life

There is a place you should visit. A journey you should take, a place where your mind, body, and soul will be in perfect harmony with the Universal Intelligence. A place where whatever you have wanted in your life can become a reality.

This journey is like taking any other exciting trip. You have a destination, that is your goal. That will be your vision. Nurture it in your thoughts. See it clearly in your mind's eye.

You will need a map of the route you will take. That will be your plan. Increase your knowledge of what you want out of life. Look for the different ways or routes you can take to get there. Pick the one you will enjoy the most.

You will need a capable and solid vehicle. That will be you. Look for and acquire the strengths that would benefit you on your journey.

You'll need to trust your vehicle's capabilities. That will be your faith and belief in yourself and in the Universal Force that is part of you and at your disposal.

You will need the fuel to keep your engine moving forward. That will be what motivates you, your inspiration, and your commitment. Don't hesitate any longer. Start your journey today

269. Helping vs. Empowering

There is a right way and a wrong way to help or assist others in conquering a situation or achieving a goal. It is better to empower someone than to help them. What may at first seem as harsh or tough words or approach from a friend, parent, mentor or trainer, can often times be better in the long run for the receiver and their self-esteem as well as for the giver

270. That Special You

We all have different qualities, talents and gifts which we can use in life. We are all in different situations and circumstances, but we all possess the same potential and capabilities to improve and rise to higher levels. Don't compare yourself to others. Carefully seek out and discover what you have at your disposal that you can use to help yourself as well as others to conquer your personal goals and achieve your true purpose. Sink all of your commitment into that. We must take responsibility for doing the best we can with what we have individually been given in our lives.

271. Dilemma

The duality in the way that the negative and positive aspects of the yin-yang express themselves in our thoughts can cause confusion and doubt. Half of you want things to work out in your favor, and the other half worries that they won't. You think, work for, and imagine a positive outcome, but you also think your optimism and positive outlook will not produce the desired effect.

If your subconscious fear and pessimism is stronger than your conscious efforts and optimism, you will never reach your goal, and your life will remain the same. Always believe in the possibility of success.

272. Visualization

I strongly believe, and always advocate, the power of thought and visualization to create new circumstances, with business, art, anything tangible, in training your athletic physical abilities or in your life.

There has been extensive research that supports the idea of how linking visualization tremendously improves motivation, confidence and performance as well as the quality of the final action, product or results.

273. An Invisible Fuel

Day by day, we need to put forth steadfastly a hidden yet positive energy by being committed, patient, and strongly believe that our lives will reach the goals, objectives and the meaningful purpose we each individually yearn for and desire for ourselves and loved ones.

274. Another Day another Lesson

When something goes wrong in your life don't ask why, ask what. What am I supposed to learn from this?

Although you may not understand how you know that you know that you know you will indure, survive and move forward to greater things. And that this lesson will help you see the invisible, feel the intangible and achieve the impossible.

275. A Universal Essence

From the beginning of time, all humans and animals have felt hunger. Something intrinsic in our minds and bodies makes us realize we need to eat. Even though a lot of people, because of ignorance and lack of knowledge, have died from what they eat, and others get sick because they eat the wrong things or in excess, it doesn't take away the notion from our minds that we each have of the need to eat.

Spirituality is the same. It is the foundation of being inspired, or being "in spirit" to achieve, to grow, prosper and succeed at everything we do. As we observe the universe, nature, and all living things, we realize there's a greater force than we that makes things happen and keeps this world in perpetual motion

Although so many, through a practice of "religions" have bastardized, misinterpreted, abused, killed, and tortured others for self-interest, personal gain or power, it doesn't take away this feeling that we have of trying to discover, explain to ourselves, or tap into this greater force. Don't discount or ignore these feelings that you experience. But also don't take anyone else's explanation, stories or theories of how you should interpret this human instinct and need. Go out and observe this nature, the ocean, the mountains, and all things. Visit a church, or synagogues, ignore the other people, their interpretations, and their reactions. Think for yourself. Feel in your own heart, mind and soul what moves you, what inspires you, what makes you feel at one with this universal essence May the force be with you.

276. Mind Strength

Reading is to the mind what exercise is to the body, your two greatest possessions, your mind and your body. Invest time in both of them.

277. Plant Your Seeds

Your mind is the fertile ground- Your dreams are the seed-
Your motivation is the fertilizer- Your hard work is the
cultivation- Your success is the fruit.

278. Bit by Bit

Every great achievement and success you reach your life is comprised and will come about in small daily increments of victories as well as failures.

279. Inner Peace

Do not let the conflicts and turmoil that surround you destroy the inner peace you can find and nurture within you.

280. You Are The Force

Having a strong unshakeable belief that you are part of a Universal Force, intelligence and wisdom will give you a calm, confident demeanor that will be seen by everyone you encounter and will help you exude the strength and energy you will need to courageously face and overcome the obstacles or challenges and enable you to reach the success you seek in your life."